The Life And Times Of Joe J. Flynn

Written by

Sandra Flynn Camburn

Copyright © *Sandra F. Camburn*, 2025

All Rights Reserved

This book is subject to the condition that no part of this book is to be reproduced, transmitted in any form or means; electronic or mechanical, stored in a retrieval system, photocopied, recorded, scanned, or otherwise. Any of these actions require the proper written permission of the author.

Contents

INTRODUCTION 1
ACKNOWLEDGEMENTS 3
DEDICATION 4

CHAPTER ONE Once Young 5
CHAPTER TWO U.S. Marine 20
CHAPTER THREE The Big Rock Candy Mountain 26
CHAPTER FOUR Merchant Ships 36
CHAPTER FIVE Easy does It 54
CHAPTER SIX A New World Opening Up   71
CHAPTER SEVEN Living Life to the Fullest 91
CHAPTER EIGHT A Fading Full Moon 102

Joe's Newspaper Articles   109

Joe Flynn's Memorial   123

Talk delivered by son-in-law, Nick 124
Talk delivered by son, John, at church service 127
Valerie shared this reading and then some of her memories. 129
The Desiderata 130
Winifred read this passage from Ecclesiastes 3:1-8 132

BIBLIOGRAPHY 133

The Life And Times Of Joe J. Flynn

The true story of a boy brought up on the streets of New York City during the Great Depression. He had ambition and an enthusiasm for life that just wouldn't quit. He had a faith in God that held his life together in the worst of times. He fought poverty and alcoholism, raised eight children and became a million dollar salesman. Joe lived a remarkable life which embraced poverty, addiction, survival, love and success. He took nothing for granted, living life with a self-driven purpose and determination.

INTRODUCTION

Dad asked me to help him write his story after his voice had already started to fade due to Parkinson Disease. At times, it was very hard to understand him. Sometimes it was impossible, but I didn't want to keep interrupting him so I'd let him go till his thoughts came around again, making more sense. Along with not always being able to understand all he was saying, he left parts of his adventures out. The parts of his life he wasn't proud of. Dad wasn't one to dwell on mistakes. His idea of life was to just keep moving forward. The old live and learn spirit. We've all been there; we just want to talk about our successes not our short comings. It is part of being human. He knew also his first audience was his family and who doesn't want to be a hero in their own family?

It has taken me years to connect the dots, so to speak; even more years to sit down and put his life story all together. I felt I had to write this story primarily because Dad asked me to, but also because there is a bit of that fighting Irish spirit in all of us. In Dad's life that spirit went against him for a while, but he managed to bring it around full swing and build a very prolific life, a life to thank God for and be proud of. Dad's life example, positive attitude, philosophies and teachings have influenced all of our lives. I am sharing with each of you the details I have learned from Dad, from Mom, from his writings, from old military records, old letters he wrote, his mother wrote, his father wrote, and his brother wrote, and hours and hours of research.

It has been twenty-three years since Dad died. Every winter, when life slows down a little here on the farm, I'd get a few more ideas and do more research. This year Dad's story started to come all together. I wanted to understand more about the life of a man, his family loved and respected, and how he influenced our lives. I can honestly say, I've enjoyed every bit of the journey. Dad believed life was for living and that he did to the fullest!

ACKNOWLEDGEMENTS

With appreciation, I'd like to acknowledge the generous assistance and advice from the following individuals-

My friends at the Writer's Group in Tunkhannock, especially Brenda Fager, Shawn Galvin, Lydia Callwitts, and John Matson.

My good friend, Sue Sill, who really knows her way around a computer and would help in any way she could.

My brothers and sisters for helping me to fill in some of the details I missed.

My husband, John, who is always ready to give me, his encouragement and support.

My daughter, Cheri, and my granddaughter, Emily, who would help me out when documents became "lost" on my computer.

My dad and mom for all the memories they left with me.

And my dad for asking me to do this project and having enough faith in me to get it done - At times I was clearly in over my head.

As dad signed his letters, Be of Good Cheer

Thank You,

    Blessings to you all, Sandi

DEDICATION

This book is dedicated to my Dad.

Dad felt it was so very important for people to understand their mistakes, learn from them and realize that your mistakes don't define your life. He felt that one should just keep on striving to do things better, and know that God has a plan for your life. Things will come together for good if given the chance.

"This life is a test. It is only a test. If it was an actual life you would have received further instructions on where to go and what to do."

(One of Dad's favorites but the author is unknown)

CHAPTER ONE
Once Young

Joseph Ignatius Flynn was born on August 30, 1917 in Plainfield, New Jersey. To tell you his story, I first have to acquaint you with his parents, Winifred Kilcullen and John Flynn.

Winifred was born in Ireland on September 1, 1885 in Cloonakeemogue County near Sligo, Ireland. In Ireland, between 1845 and 1852, in just seven years, one million Irish people perished from starvation and disease; two million more escaped death through emigration during that time. A potato blight destroyed the potato crops that were the primary, often only, food for most of Ireland's inhabitants causing a severe famine. British misgovernment (Ireland didn't become independent of England until 1922) and landlord tyranny stripped the common people of their land and homes. Economic distress, religious persecution and political unrest all oppressed the poor Irish man. Between 1841 and 1920, Ireland's population fell from about eight million to about four million people.

Young children were brought up being told that America was the land where there was "work and food for all"; they should go, for there was nothing but starvation and death left in Ireland. Emigrating from Ireland to America was fraught with difficulty and danger but many Irish saw no alternative. They would have to spend two months in cold, damp and cramped quarters aboard ships. Sickness and disease can spread rampantly in those conditions. During the late 1800's and early 1900's, Irish female immigrants far outnumbered the males. This was in sharp contrast to the overwhelmingly male migrations from southern and eastern Europe.

In Winifred's family the oldest sister, Mary, came across the Atlantic first when she turned eighteen. She worked a few years and sent money back to her family for the next sister to come across. Margaret came next, and then Winifred came to America in 1903, when she turned eighteen. Bridget, the youngest sister came across the ocean a year or two later. This was referred to as "chain migration".

On the ship rosters, all those on board were listed. In this way, they could keep track of all the people on board for some died before they reached America. Many Irish were listed, including Winifred, as servants. Others were listed as dressmakers, laborers and farmers. Winifred's brother, John, escorted her to the ship. She had thirty dollars on her when she left Queenstown, Ireland. When her ship docked at Ellis Island, she had to report to the port authorities to be cleared to enter the United States. Her sister, Maggie, met Winifred at the docks. Maggie was her sponsor. One had to have a sponsor to come to the United States. Your sponsor would give you room and board until you could secure a job and provide for yourself, there was no government assistance.

Winifred's brother, John, stayed in Ireland to help on the parent's farm. In Ireland, they may have referred to their land as a farm, but virtually it was a land lot not more than a quarter acre. It was a practice to have one son stay behind in Ireland to help support the parents. There was no government help for poor families. If the father died, the wife and children were evicted from their cottage. They were thrown out into the elements. The Irish people called this period "an Gorta Mor" (uh GOR-tuh more)- "the Great Hunger". They were told by the government that the son left to care for the parents shouldn't marry till his parents died. John did eventually marry and did have children.

Neither John, nor his parents ever came to America. Mary, Margaret, Winifred and Bridget never went back to Ireland.

The majority of Irish women in America around the turn of the century spent five to ten years working as servants in large households. Servants rarely suffered unemployment and room and board were provided. They could save their little earnings. There was a lot of religious prejudice and social prejudice, the Irish had to deal with here in the United States at that time. Many of the woman dreamed of getting married and having their own home. Unfortunately, marriage to a working class Irishman often meant that his wife and children would have to endure poverty and the insecurity resulting from his low wages, frequent unemployment and drunken abuse. Most Irish immigrants, however, were grateful to the United States for giving them the chance to have liberties and opportunities denied them in Ireland.

Winifred liked living in New York City. She was happy to be near Mary and Margaret, and their families. Bridget lived in New Jersey for a time but then moved to California. Bridget didn't keep in touch with her sisters.

After working in New York for thirteen years, and still not finding a husband, Winifred decided to travel to Ohio to visit a nun she knew, living in a convent out there. Maybe thoughts of joining the convent went through her head due to her situation in life.

If she had such thoughts, they were soon forgotten when she met John Joseph Flynn. He was handsome, exciting and knew how to show a pretty girl a good time. Winifred was smitten from the get- go.

John Joseph Flynn was born in Cincinnati, Ohio on July 19, 1890 to Irish immigrant parents, Martin Flynn and Delia Manion Flynn. He was the youngest of thirteen children. His parents ran a four story boarding house with a grocery store and bar on the street level.

John was a hyperactive child. He told stories about when he was a child. "When I was old enough to walk my mom would put me in a tub which sat on the kitchen floor to wash me. If I was left alone I'd jump out of that tub and run out into the street like the sun shines (with nothing on) just to get people to react". John claimed he was the wildest kid in Cincinnati. "I'd sneak out of the house in the morning and more than once, the police would find me having a little fun, and take me home."

At the age of six he was confined to bed for almost a year due to severe burns he received when he ignited toy caps with boiler slugs. "I was nearly burnt up alive!" he'd recall. "I had to learn to walk all over again and the pain was horrific!" Eighty years later he still had scars on his legs. On the one leg the scar was nine inches long and six inches wide, as an adult!

John's mom died when he was seven years old. He said his mom was loved by all the neighbors for she was kind, generous and had the Irish wit. John thought that was why he had such a good sense of humor. However, not everyone appreciated his sense of humor.

Winifred married John on December 2, 1916, three months after they met in Cincinnati, Ohio. Winifred was very vain and more than a bit superstitious. She knew she was older than John but didn't want him to know. She was thirty-one when they were married, he was twenty-six. On the marriage certificate she said she was twenty-three. Winifred was of the notion the husband should always be older than the wife in a marriage. She also stated she was a stenographer. Maybe to her that job carried a bit more class than being a waitress or maid. John said he was a masseur at the time, though he never did that line of work after they were married. Soon after they were married, they headed to Plainfield, New Jersey. Winifred missed her sisters and John liked the sounds of life near the big city.

John did some boxing to earn cash. He was good at it, feisty, quick and always ready to taunt someone. John was also very mechanically inclined and at one time owned a taxi cab license. A taxi cab license was worth quite a bit of money and gave the owner the opportunity to earn a good living. It was an opportunity John failed to take advantage of. He was more interested in socializing and drinking. Could be the reason he lost his taxi cab license a few years later.

Their first child, Joseph Ignatius Flynn, was born the following August in Plainfield, New Jersey. His brother, John James Flynn, was born two years later. By the time the kids were six and four, Winifred had enough of the drinking and moved into New York City with the boys.

Winifred and John just had very different ideas about life. Winifred had little formal education, was very protective of her children, very vain, and fearful of so many things. She would panic at the sight of small animals like dogs or cats. She thought they carried disease. She was afraid of the elevators in the department stores. She didn't want to be closed into such a small place. John, on the other hand, would tease her about such things. He was adventurous, belligerent, had an explosive personality and loved to drink.

It was hard raising two boys in the city by herself. She worked in hotels, as a maid or worked in restaurants as a waitress. She did the best she could to put food on the table, and keep the bills paid. When she had no money to pay the rent, she'd move. John was no help. He'd show up to see the boys and take them to the garage to play while he worked on the vehicles. The boys would return home covered in dirt and grease. She was so upset with him, and he'd see nothing wrong with how they spent the day or the dirty disheveled mess their clothes were in. To him, the boys had fun, it didn't matter that they were filthy dirty. Sometimes he'd leave the boys sleep in the cab while he drank. One time John got into a street fight. The police came broke it up and took

Joe's dad to jail, not realizing the boys were in the garage, hiding in a car. Young Joe was always very self –sufficient, and figured out how to get him and his brother home. Winifred tried to keep John away from the boys, but sooner or later, he would find them.

Winifred and her boys were never in one apartment long. Either Winifred couldn't pay the rent and was asked to leave, or the old man was bothering her, and she'd move to get away from him. Joe said he couldn't remember passing a grade. Every time his mom moved, he'd start at a new school. The teacher would ask how old he was and put him in the appropriate grade.

Joe saved a letter from the Social Service Department stating that Joe and his brother needed dental care but Mrs. Flynn being the sole support of the family could not afford to pay the clinic fee. The letter states that she worked as a waitress and earned an average of seven dollars a week in 1928. The East side of New York where they lived was called "hell's kitchen". Times were tough. The Great Depression had set in. As a kid Joe was happy, he never knew any other way of living. He was ambitious and had a real positive attitude.

Joe took on odd jobs as soon as he could. He shined shoes on street corners, and sold Hershey Bars in Union Square. He sold newspapers in the streets or in the subways.

Joe canvassed diligently to get subscriptions for the Brooklyn Eagle. He became a star newspaper boy, and was awarded from time to time with baskets of food and chickens. His mom really appreciated them and prepared meals for Joe and his brother, Jack. The Brooklyn Eagle even gave Joe a second paper route, which he let his brother, Jack, take over.

As a teenager, Joe had a job delivering telegrams on his second hand bike to offices on Wall Street for two cents per telegram. "I made one and half dollars in a day, some days," he'd state positively. "I like to work and I know how to make a buck". Joe was sure of that. He hung on to that job till he was seventeen.

In his early teens Joe came up with another idea to earn money. He and his brother built a wagon from scrap wood and old wheels. The boys got help to buy two cases of beer with an alcoholic content of one and a half percent, all that the Prohibition laws allowed at the time. They put the beer on ice, in the wagon, and took it down to the construction sites on the west side of Manhattan. They sold it to the workers near quitting time. Some of the workers were working on building high- rise buildings, and others were building the subway. The boys bought the beer for eight cents a bottle and sold it for twenty cents a bottle. Joe and Jack sold all sixty bottles the first day. When their dad heard of their success, he bought what he needed to make his own beer to sell. Unfortunately, he became his own best customer.

Good times came when Joe's mom would take him, and his brother to visit one of her sisters, their aunts. It was the best time visiting the cousins. They would all play together,and were always welcome to stay, and sleep on the floor. There was food to eat at their house and Aunt Mary would give Joe and Jack each a nickel or maybe even a dime.

Soon Joe reached his teen years. Joe dropped out of school after eighth grade graduation to deliver telegrams which he could only do during the day when the offices were open. He did this to help support his mom and brother. His mom's waitressing job just wasn't enough for all three of them during the depression. Sometimes she'd get extra work cleaning rooms in the hotel. It was just a very hard time for everyone.

Joe's cousin enlisted in the service. This sounded like a great idea to Joe. He wanted to join the Marines to see the world, and have a steady job. He would have money sent home to his mother to help her with food and rent. Maybe his brother, Jack, would follow him into the service when he became old enough to join. His mom was thinking the Marines would keep Joe off the streets and out of trouble. She signed his papers so he could join the Marines at seventeen years old. Joe was off on an adventure.

John and Winifred with infant Joseph 1917

Father John with sons Joseph and Jack 1920

Joseph 1924

Brothers Joseph and Jack 1926

CHAPTER TWO
U.S. Marine

Joe enlisted in the U.S. Marine Corps on September 5, 1934. For some unknown reason his enlistment papers were made out in the name of Joseph Bernard Flynn. He signed them that way and so did his mother. At seventeen years old he stood five feet seven inches and weighed one hundred thirty-seven pounds. He was enlisted as a private to learn drum and trumpet probably because of his size. He was a very willing worker and he tried hard to learn to play the trumpet. Seven months later he was let go from the field music school. They called him "two note Flynn". Joe just couldn't grasp the fundamentals of music in order to learn to play the trumpet.

Joe requalified as a rifle sharp shooter, a pistol marksman, a bayonet expert and scored excellent on the grenade course. He was well developed physically considering his age and size. The Marine Corp determined he was fit for general service.

For almost two years he seemed to be adjusting to life as a Marine and coping well with all that was required of him. Joe was stationed on the east coast, at Parris Island for almost a year. He was then assigned to the Norfolk Navy Shipyard in Portsmouth, Virginia where he was involved in building, repairing and remodeling the Navy's ships. The Marine Corps is technically a part of the U.S. Navy although both the Navy and Marine Corp are regarded as separate branches of the military.

After Portsmouth, Joe was stationed at Quantico, Virginia, until he received orders to go to San Diego, California. He was stationed at Camp Pendleton in San Diego when the Marine Corps transferred him into 2nd chemical Company, Second Marine Brigade. After seven months at the base he was stationed on the U.S.S. Texas which was the most decorated ship in the

U.S. Navy fleet at the time. He sailed the west coast and the Hawaiian Islands. He liked the traveling and the sailing but he started having trouble following orders and obeying the rules didn't seem to be on his mind.

Joe's first offence on July 15, 1936 was hitch-hiking in the city of San Diego, in uniform, for which he did ten hours of public works. For the next six months he carried on as ordered but soon things went arye. He started drinking.

In February of 1937 Joe was AOL (absent over leave) for two days. He was court martialed and sentenced to confinement for six days and fined seven dollars of his pay for that month.

In April 1937, he was found drunk, disorderly and fighting ashore. For that episode he was given two weeks restriction by his C.O. (commissioned officer).

In early May, Joe disobeyed orders and skipped duty. He was given a three day confinement punishment by the C.O. His commissioned officer was trying to get him back on track.

Joe was on the U.S.S. Texas in the Pacific Ocean right off the coast of San Francisco, California on May 27, 1937 where he witnessed one of the grandest events of his life. This grand event was also Joe's excuse, as if he had to have one, for skipping duty. The longest and tallest suspension bridge in the world, The Golden Gate Bridge, which took five years to construct, was opening up. Eleven men died during the construction of the bridge. Nineteen more fell off the scaffolding and were caught by the safety net below the bridge. It was said they joined the Halfway-to Hell Club for that was quite the fall but all of the men survived. Its tallest towers were 746 feet high and it was nearly two miles long (9000 feet). The celebrating lasted a week. The city of San Francisco closed offices, stores, and schools. They declared a holiday. The opening day of the celebrations was called Pedestrian's Day and no vehicles were allowed on the bridge. Eighty thousand people were lined up to be among the first to cross the bridge. At six in the morning on May 27, 1937 fog horns blasted, the bridge gates were opened and the celebrations began.

There were marching bands, floats and dignitaries in the parades. People crossed on stilts, roller skates, unicycles and bikes. Some tap danced across or walked their animals across. There was a group of men playing harmonics all the way across. It was a grand party and the men on ship, who had never seen anything like this celebrated too, they just wanted to be involved. There were two hundred thousand people in the city for the festivities that week.

There were good times in the military and being in the Marines had its advantages. When Joe started drinking he just didn't seem to recognize any good in military life or any advantages to being a Marine. He could only drink and just didn't think.

In July 1937 Joe and his buddy Otto J. Westfall skipped duty on the U.S.S. Texas and were AOL for five days. They hitch hiked across the country to the Marine Base in Philadelphia, Pennsylvania and turned themselves in. After appearing in Deck Court they were put in confinement for twenty days. Joe was serving his last day in the brig when one of the guards gave him an order. Joe probably thought he was getting bossed around and didn't like it. He started running his mouth and told the guard he had "a wild hair up his ass". The guard reported the incident to the captain.

On August 4, 1937 Joe was court martialed. The court ruled he was using provoking words toward another person in the U.S. Navel Service. The court went over his records and now with this new development it didn't go well for Joe. He was sentenced to a Bad Conduct Discharge from The United States Marine Corps.

Joe had a lot of common sense but he still had a lot of that street kid in him. He would get bold, mouthy and belligerent especially when he had been drinking. He felt he was above the law and authority. He felt his superior officers were jackasses. The biggest problem being he didn't mind telling them so.

Joe's buddy Otto and another young man, Mike, were discharged on the same day. The three men decided to go out west together. To them at this stage of their game a Bad Conduct Discharge or B.C.D. just meant Big Chicken Dinner! (slang the guys used in that situation to make lite of it- though there was nothing lite about it). This term probably came from the fact that their good sense went a foul.

two-note Flynn

Joe qualified as a rifle sharp shooter

Joe and fellow Marines

The Marine Boxers

C.D. Green, Company D and J.B. Flynn, Chemical Company, decision.

CHAPTER THREE
The Big Rock Candy Mountain

Footloose and fancy free, so to speak, the three men, not really realizing the gravity of all that had just happened with their military careers, thought they were in the right and had just won their "freedom". They decided to go to Idaho after being released from the Marine barracks in Philadelphia.

With little money, in their pockets, they hopped a freight train going to Buffalo. In Buffalo they changed trains and hopped one headed to Indianapolis. As luck would have it the three hobos were caught by the train guards.

They were transported to the local jail and put in a cell with another inmate. The guys got to talking with this fellow inmate. Come to find out, their fellow inmate was in jail for killing his father. This revelation alone made the guys a bit uncomfortable. Never thought they'd land in jail for hopping trains much less with a person who committed murder.

The other thing that startled them was the giant cockroaches running around on the jail- house floor. "Hell, those dam things are two inches long!" complained Otto.

The young fellas were more than a little agitated by this whole jail situation. Mike, Joe's other buddy, sent a letter home to ask for help. His family sent ten dollars. That was enough money to get all three guys out of jail with a bit left over.

They were out of jail and on the journey again. The boys took off to find the nearest train station, and waited away from the station, where they wouldn't be so likely to be spotted by the train guards, and hopped on a freight train headed for Montana. In Montana, the three of them took jobs on a farm picking potatoes. It was hard work, hard on their backs and legs. The food they were given was good, but the bed bugs were terrible. At first, they were just itchy, but after a few nights their whole bodies were covered with bites. The boys decided to move on to Colorado.

They found themselves outside of a small town called Cripple Creek, Colorado. They were about twenty miles southwest of Colorado Springs near the base of Pike's Peak when they met an old guy who was panning for gold along the river. The old guy was happy to share food and drink with the boys. They all sat around a campfire, and the prospector told them about the past in Cripple Creek.

In a deep husky voice he told them, "The last great Colorado gold rush began when a rich ore was found in 1890. Cripple Creek was considered no more than cattle pasture then, with a population of about four or five hundred at that time. That damn gold rush brought in about seven or eight hundred more people by the end of the 1890's, and by the end of 1892, Cripple Creek was home to more than five thousand people, with another five thousand in nearby towns! By 1910, the miners had mined 22.4 million ounces of gold, making it the fourth most prosperous town in Colorado, at the time."

The old prospector liked to talk and he had a good audience. He talked about how the sheriff and his boys confiscated all the guns from the newcomers who came into town. "No guns were allowed in town," he said. "The sheriff didn't want no trouble, and the sheriff needed money. So, he would sell the guns in Denver, and the money was used to pay teachers. You have to realize now, that there were almost four thousand young folks in town then, and they needed an education. There was a college, nineteen schools, and about one hundred eighty teachers. That's why they needed that money from selling the guns."

"Now let me tell you", the old man continued, "during that gold boom, if I can remember, there were one hundred fifty saloons, forty-nine grocery stores, twenty-five restaurants, four pretty good size department stores, twelve casinos, and thirty-four churches in the town." "Town also had ninety doctors, forty stockbrokers, who were out to swindle anyone who struck gold, fifteen newspapers, and seventy- two lawyers. It also had ten barber shops, and twenty houses of ill-repute, with about three hundred prostitutes. There were madams, to take care of the prostitution business in each of the houses. Those houses of prostitution flourished until the 1920's and were taxed at a rate of six dollars a month for each one of them there girls. The madams had to each pay sixteen dollars in taxes each month. Oh, and there were a bunch of opium dens. It was a wild place to be in the late eighteen hundreds and early nineteen hundreds."

He had stories of a lynching that took place in town. He then told the tale of a miner fighting with his girl at the saloon. The old prospector said, "In his rage that miner grabbed an oil lantern. He was so mad he threw it across the room. The lantern smashed, and set the curtains on fire. The buildings were all wood, and there was no fire department. That fire spread so quickly, it incinerated all the wooden buildings on that side of the road, before it was put out."

He went on to say, "And I heard tell, that it wasn't more than a week later a cook in the hotel spilled a kettle of grease on a hot stove which started a fire that spread and burned down one third of Cripple Creek. Today (1939) Cripple Creek has mostly reverted back to a "ghost" town. It has about, maybe, a thousand people."

The guys loved visiting and listening to the experienced prospector tell stories. They sure enjoyed the food and drink but they had to move on.

They headed to Idaho. Joe and Otto found work in a restaurant. The boss offered them food, a bed, and a little cash for their help. They thought that was a good deal for the two of them. Joe tried his hand at being a cook. He enjoyed cooking and found he had a knack for short order cooking.

Mike was hired by a carpenter, he met. He decided to stay in Idaho when the other guys wanted to move on. They said their good-byes and Joe and Otto headed toward California and up towards Seattle, Washington.

Well, after a few weeks, this idea of seeing the world as hobos was more than they bargained for and not quite what they expected. The life was hard, at times, and so unpredictable; cold rainy weather and no food to count on. "The Big Rock Candy Mountain" was one of Joe's favorite hobo songs.

The Hobo's Song - Big Rock Candy Mountains

One evening as the sun went down and the jungle fires were burning, down the track came an old hobo hiking, He said, "Boys I'm not turning , I'm headed for a land that's far away beside the crystal fountain. So come with me, we'll go see the Big Rock Candy Mountain."

In the Big Rock Candy Mountain it's a land that's fair and bright. The handouts grow on bushes and you sleep out every night. The boxcars all are empty and the sun shines every day. Oh, the birds and the bees, and the cigarette trees. The lemonade springs where the bluebird sings In the Big Rock Candy Mountain.

In the Big Rock Candy Mountains the cops have wooden legs. The bulldogs all have rubber teeth and the hens lay soft boiled eggs. The farmer's trees are full of fruit and the barns are full of hay. Oh, I'm bound to go where there ain't no snow, where the rain don't fall, where the wind don't blow In the Big Rock Candy Mountains.

In the Big Rock Candy Mountain you never change your socks and little streams of alky-hol come trickling down the rocks. Oh, the brakemen have to tip their hats and the railroad bulls are blind. There's a lake of stew and of whiskey too, you can paddle around in a big canoe. In the Big Rock Candy Mountains.

In the Big rock Candy Mountains the jails are made of tin. You can slip right out again as soon as you walk in. There ain't no short-handled shovels, no axes, saws or picks. I'm goin' to stay, Where you sleep all day, Where they hung the jerk that invented work, in the Big Rock Candy Mountains. I'll see you all this coming fall In the Big Rock Candy Mountains.

Written and sung by Harry McClintock (1928)

The hobos were getting nowhere fast, and they were not finding "The Big Rock Candy Mountain." Joe and Otto were always hungry, always feeling grubby, always wondering where they'd be if it started to rain, sleet or snow. They decided to go to Louisiana where Otto's family had a farm; at least they'd have a roof over their heads providing a warm, dry place, to eat and sleep.

It was quite a trip and, of course, between the two of them they were broke. In their travels they passed a bakery where they asked for work. The owner had no work. So the guys asked for some stale bread, they were very hungry. The owner of the bakery threw them out, he thought they were too persistent, they must be trouble. "Persistence is a good thing to me" said Joe to himself.

Hopping trains was their main mode of transportation, and they always ran the risk of getting caught by the train guards. It was a long, long trip home.

When they finally reached Otto's family's farm, his mom had prepared a big meal for the young men. They were both so very hungry, they stuffed themselves. Not a good idea. They both experienced extreme sickness. Their stomachs couldn't handle the amount of food they tried to eat after going without food for so long.

Joe stayed at Otto's farm helping out doing odd jobs for a while. He spent his time cutting sugar cane, picking cotton, tattooing the pigs, and working with the mules. You can bet by the end of the week they were out on the town drinking.

While working out in the sugar cane fields, Joe developed blisters on his feet. His footwear was shot. The blisters became infected, making it hard to walk. Joe wrote his mother a letter explaining his predicament. She sent him the proceeds from his cancelled Marine Corps life insurance policy that had been sent to her, two dollars and four cents. It was enough to get him home to his mother's apartment in New York City.

Joe stayed with his mom while his feet healed. Soon after his feet felt better he looked his dad and brother up. Once he was in contact with them, they were all out drinking.

Joe's dad rented a cold water flat with four rooms for twenty dollars a month. The bathroom was down the hallway. It was a community bathroom. All the tenants on the floor shared one bathroom.

The old man, Joe, and his brother, Jack, would get rowdy after drinking, which was never appreciated by the other tenants. Not a one of them had a job at the time. The rent was being neglected. The land-lord wanted his money and one day he was hollering so loud everyone in the whole apartment building could hear him. Joe asked his mother to borrow some cash to pay the rent. Winifred helped them out, but she made it clear, this was a one-time deal. She, too, was struggling, and she didn't have any more money to loan them. It was hard finding work during the depression, but that's exactly what they had to do or live in the streets. Winifred was the only Flynn working. She had a waitress job not too far from her apartment.

One night after drinking, John, the old man, decided to stop over at Winifred's apartment. Winifred had a male friend over. John started with the mouth, bullying the man, then threating him. A fight broke out between the two. John grabbed an iron bar from the corner, and wacked it across the man's arm. Winifred had called the police already and they got John out of her apartment but he had already broken the man's arm. John was arrested.

It was after that incident that John decided to leave New York. He went to San Francisco, joined the painter's union there and made a new life for himself. Winifred and John never divorced legally and never saw each other again, until thirty years later.

Joe needed a job badly. The depression was still going on. New York City was one of the cities most affected. There were fifty community eating rooms just on the lower east side of the city, where Joe lived. Most of the big factories were still closed. One in three men was unemployed. Women and children were being abandoned by men who couldn't support them. There was a lack of heating, and hot water in the apartments. Crimes increased in the city, children couldn't attend school and the middle class had no money, and no security. At the same time, the United States was on the verge of another war. Fighting had already begun in Europe, England and Japan. Joe wrote a letter to his Major General in the Marine Corps asking to be reinstated in the United States Marines.

Brooklyn New York
Febuary 20, 1938

Maj Gen, Com,
Unith States Marines

Sir
    Writing you in regard to reinstaten in the Unith States Marines.

    I was dismass from the service on Aug 13, 1937. At the Philadelphia Navy Yard. With a Bad Conduct Discharge.

    Since that time I leaned my mistake.

Wishing my record lookup I am sure you will fine that I did my soldering well.

    I would also like to call your attenet to my age. I was seventeen when enlisted. And knowing little or nothing of the outside world. And being ove. anquish to get out. I have made the mistake of loseing my head at the wrong time

Erkening the service for one

> more chance which I know I am not worthy of. But would like to prove to the officers and men of the service that I am worthy of being one of them.
>
> Hoping the letter brings back a satisfactory reply.
>
> I remain at your service.
>
> Yours so Truly
> Joseph B. Flynn
> Ex Pvt. U.S.M.C
>
> address 3903 - 3rd Ave
> Brooklyn N.Y.

The letter was very well written, for a guy with only an eighth grade education. Joe had a sharp mind, but he still didn't recognize he had a problem with alcohol. He knew he had to find work.

The Marine Corps Director of Personal did respond to Joe's letter but not favorably.

245413
AP-36-wjs

24 February 1938.

My dear Mr. Flynn:

The receipt is acknowledged of your letter of February 20th, requesting permission to reenlist in the Marine Corps, waiving the fact that you were last discharged with a Bad Conduct Discharge.

It is a policy of the Marine Corps not to accept for reenlistment any man who was last discharged under other than honorable conditions, in view of which, your reenlistment in the Marine Corps can not consistently be authorized.

Sincerely yours,

JULIAN C. SMITH,
Colonel, U. S. M. C.,
Director of Personnel.

Mr. Joseph B. Flynn,
3803 - 3rd Avenue,
Brooklyn, N.Y.

Joe needed to find a job and the sooner the better.

CHAPTER FOUR
Merchant Ships

Joe heard that the Merchant Ship Companies down at the New York docks were hiring workers. That, to Joe, sounded like a great job - hard work, adventure, part of a team to transport materials, good pay, food and a bunk to sleep in.

It was like being in the military, although the Merchant Marines were not considered part of the U.S. military. Throughout the Second World War, our armed forces relied on the Merchant marines to transport supplies, cargo, and personnel into all ports of operation and they paid a heavy price in service to their country. The Merchant Marines lost more men than any other branch of the United States Services in World War II. An estimated ninety- three hundred mariners lost their lives, and another twelve thousand were wounded, to make sure our service members could keep fighting. Yet, these men who put their lives on the line as Mariners were not even given veteran status until 1988, many years too late for the 125,000 mariners who had already died. That was roughly half of those who had served their country.

During World War II, the merchant service sailed and took orders from naval officers. However, they were formally considered volunteers and not members of the military. They belonged to a National Maritime Union. The outbreak of war in Europe made the Merchant Marines significant for security and defense reasons. Joe was hired on as a civilian.

Joe went down to the shipping office to get his orders. His first trip out to sea was on the S.S. Meteor from June 28, 1938 to July5, 1938. For eight days he was in the coal passer position. The work of the coal passer was to move enormous piles of coal on the dock into coal bunkers on the ship below deck. A man could do about fifty trips a shift.

On each trip, the sailor would go to the coal pile on the dock, and fill a bucket with about one hundred pounds of coal. Then he would carry it down the stairs, in the ship to the coal bunkers.

Shoveling coal, and maintaining steam was a constant chore at sea. It was a dirty back- breaking job. A steam ship would burn eight to ten tons of coal per hour at full power. After getting the coal aboard ship and in the bunkers, clean up was essential. The ship deck was hosed down and scrubbed clean. The men, who were covered in coal dust, did not have the luxury of showers; they scrubbed off with buckets of water.

After the coal was safely stowed away, and the ship underway, the coal passers continued the thankless job of shoveling coal into the furnace. Sailor Frederick Wilson, a former coal passer described his job, as the coal passer, in his diary: "that most humble but necessary evil, the lowest rating in the service, an object that isn't supposed to be human at all, but has to delve wherever dirt and grime is thickest, in back connection, in the bilge, in mucky feed tanks, in the boiler and in the coal bunker. Poor coal Passer! Cursed and damned by all parts of the ship, whose very footprints are watched as he crosses spotless decks, who is blamed for every spot of dirt on deck and paint work as a matter of course. Like many others of humble rating, his necessity and worth goes unrecognized."

After working as the coal passer for eight days out at sea and leaving the ship with money in their pockets, the only place those men could think of going was one of the local bars. It was time to unwind. The men would say- A trip and a spree, A trip and a spree. They had to have a story for the next trip out to sea. Joe went right along with them. His next trip out was just over a week away. You can bet that's long enough to get into a bit of trouble, so as to have a story to tell on the next trip out to sea. Is there any such thing as a bit of trouble?

He was assigned to the S.S. Robin Grey for three months in the capacity of mess boy. The mess boy is the go-to guy on the ship when it comes to anything related to food, general hygiene and cleanliness. Tasks such as helping the ship's cook, setting tables, making coffee and drinks, clean mess area, wash dishes, pots and pans, gets done by the mess boy. The mess boy also makes the Officer's beds, and cleans and maintains their quarters. He was responsible for stocking and taking inventory of supplies.

Joe was learning the way of life on ship. He was part of the crew, one of the guys and the guys would drink together after ship duty, sometimes not even waiting till after ship duty. It was only his second voyage out, and about six of the guys were fired for a nice little party, they were having in the mess room. It didn't bother any of them much to be fired. There were other ships to ship out on. Joe got so he thought of himself as a "one tripper". If you get into trouble on one ship, just ship out with another shipping company next time. That wasn't so bad, you still had work, and the shipping company you were with didn't really matter.

On Joe's next five voyages, he was assigned to be the wiper. The wiper would lubricate gears, bearings and other parts of engines and motors. He would read pressure and temperature gauges, record data, assist with repairs, and machinery adjustments. The wipers are the entry level workers in the engine room. Work to be performed by the wiper is meant to create a work positive environment where sea time may be secured towards earning your seamen's license. The Merchant Marines were giving Joe a chance to better himself; he was taking every chance he could to have a good time. Things would go along smoothly in that Joe wasn't caught drinking on ship and once off, he would just continue drinking. He, unfortunately, was not able to ship out for almost two months, due to the damn drinking, just couldn't get his head on straight.

While Joe was down at the shipping office he met a young, friendly girl, Pauline. She seemed to care about him. Pauline was quite talkative and made a fuss over Joe. Of course, Joe ate the attention right up. Drinking gave him confidence and the nerve to dance or sing. They enjoyed going out together while he was home.

On November 30, 1940 he was assigned to the S.S. Robin Hood. The nature of the voyage was foreign. Joe had found work on a ship headed to Africa for three months and he was ready for an adventure. He was assigned the job of fireman/ trimmer. The fireman's role was primarily to tend to the boilers and ensure they ran efficiently. The trimmer's role was to ensure the fireman had adequate supplies of coal near at hand, while also ensuring that the trim of the ship wasn't loaded with coal unevenly. Coal bunkers ran the length of the ship, on both sides of the ship. So if coal was taken out of just one bunker at a time the ship would be unbalanced. The access points to the coal were cramped; they had to dig coal out and shovel it into wheelbarrows, then wheel them along narrow tracks back to the boiler.

All this work was done without lighting, without extractor fans for the coal dust, without air conditioning in the tropics or heating in the cold climates and with the ship moving. The men ended up battered and bruised and with coal dust in open wounds and their eyes. They would use a bandana to cover their mouth and nose. Joe worked his tail off, had a good trip and made good money, too. He never shied away from hard work. He liked to accomplish things; he liked the feeling of security that money in his pocket provided.

Just three weeks later he had the opportunity to go back to Africa on another four month voyage on the same ship. He signed on. Joe was so confident in his own abilities and he had just made this trip so he knew what to expect. He was an enthusiastic worker and knew how to get things done. He liked to help the new guys on the ship learn about the ways of the Merchant Marine.

At one of the docks in Africa he began drinking some of their spiced brands of liquor. Once he started drinking he did not stop. Joe drank so much he passed out after a time. He had a "blackout" and coming out of it found himself in hand cuffs. He soon learned the Captain had put the handcuffs on him for being out of control. Joe had no memory of the previous night of drinking. He was told he got obnoxiously mouthy, went after the second mate and a few others of the crew. The Captain chewed him out and sent him back to work. The guys chalked it up to another adventure. Joe thought to himself, "God, I must have been nuts." Never realizing it was the alcohol causing his problems, he went on drinking in other ports after the work was done. Because nothing else of consequence happened he soon forgot the whole episode. Joe never went back to that shipping company or worked on that ship again but there were plenty of other shipping companies. Like he always said, "I'm a one tripper."

Joe felt good being home so he decided to take a little time off. He visited with his mother and brought her some money to help her out.

Joe and Pauline, the shipping clerk, decided to get married though they really didn't know each other very well. Joe had been out to sea, most of the time, since they met. On September 8, 1941 they were married by a justice of the peace at 340 W.55th Street. Edward Stanton and his wife Marion Stanton witnessed the marriage. They set up residence at 542 W. 112th Street.

Pauline didn't like Joe's lifestyle of shipping out to sea and the drinking. She criticized his lifestyle continually. He didn't like her always undermining his decisions, telling him what to do and then threating to end the marriage if he didn't abide by her rules. By the end of October he had enough of the arguing, and wanted to go back to sea.

He signed up for another foreign voyage. November 13, 1941 and left for three months on the S.S. Alcoa Puritan. December 4, 5, and 6, 1941 while assigned to the 4A.M. to 8A.M. watch Joe was found to be under the influence of intoxicating liquor and thereby incapacitated for the proper performance of duty. Then on January 13, 1942 the ship's Captain charged Joe with misconduct while on duty in the Port of Spain. The Shipping Company decided to send him back early to the United States on a ship headed to Portland, Maine right after the infraction. In Portland he boarded another vessel headed to New York. He was given a stern warning by the United States Coast Guard and a six month probationary period.

While in New York he tried to make things right with Pauline, but that did not go well. Joe went to see his mother, and see how she was getting along before he went back out to sea.

Japan had bombed Pearl Harbor, which brought the United States into World War II. There were German submarines off the east coast of the United States and in the Gulf of Mexico attacking and sinking the Merchant Marine ships. The war was all around them.

On March 6th, 1942 Joe took work as the oiler on the S.S. Alcoa Partner owned by the Alcoa Aluminum Company. The vessel itself was a 5,513 gross ton freighter headed to Trinidad. They had a crew of seven officers, twenty-seven crewmen and one workaway. After unloading the supplies they brought to Trinidad the crew loaded eight thousand five hundred tons of bauxite ore onto the steam ship. Bauxite is a rock formed from a laterite soil that has been severely leached of silica and other soluble materials in a wet tropical or sub-tropical climate. It is the primary ore of aluminum. The S.S. Alcoa Partner was loaded with the ore and sailing in the Caribbean Sea back to Mobile, Alabama, unarmed and unescorted.

Three years of sailing on the seas had taught Joe what a busting boiler sounded like or most any other peace time catastrophic noise that could occur on ship. He never heard a noise like he did that night when a U-66 German submarine fired one torpedo at the Alcoa Partner. This one torpedo struck the Alcoa Partner on the port side in and around the #2 hole. Since the U-66 was on the surface of the ocean waters she immediately fired off another shell, from her deck gun, which struck the steam ship in her poop deck area. Joe knew immediately that they were in serious trouble. The ship started to tip. Bedlam was running rampant. The sea was in his blood and Joe had weathered storms before but this was a kind of storm you couldn't attempt to master. You can only run away from a torpedoed ship.

The explosion had knocked out the lights and blackness was all around them; the dark deck, the dark water and the dark sky. The companionway was jammed with men running, all of them headed for the ladder leading to the upper deck and the life boats.

The lightning instinct of experience in an emergency situation guided the bosun's (slang for boatswain- a petty officer in charge of the ship's deck crew, rigging, anchors and cables) feet in the opposite direction, to where the life raft was rigged. At the exit two young men were hiding. Theoretically, every one of the men aboard ship had acquired the basic essentials of seamanship. For some though, whatever they learned seemed to evaporate in the salt breezes when put to the actual test. The bosun shouted at them in a really rough, loud voice, "The program says run, do not walk to the nearest exit!" The two young men jumped up and ran behind him. One of the men already running asked, "What are you huddled there for?"

The young men gulped, "We thought if we waited a little the ladder wouldn't be so crowded." One of the other men retorted, "They sure won't be, they'll be a mile under the water."

Joe heard the splash as the raft hit the water. The men started vaulting over the side. The first young man clambered up the side of the ship and balanced there on the rail teetering. Joe's hand descended on his shoulder and gave him a push in the right direction, off the ship. It was going down and fast. The guy gave a squawk and somersaulted down to land in a tangle of flailing arms and legs on the raft below. In a moment Joe jumped over the side of the ship and was down in the raft beside him. The young guy, who had just landed on the life raft on his knees, started yelling, "How do we unfasten that thing?" He lunged himself back toward the sinking ship. Not understanding what he was saying, Joe tried to grab his leg to prevent him from falling into the sea. He was screaming, "Frankie, I'm coming." There, halfway down the side of the ship his buddy was tangled in a rope. But before Joe could grab him, quick as a wink the young guy on the raft seized his buddy, tangled in the rope, by his belt and cut him free with a big knife, the captain had told him more than once to get rid of. With his other hand he hauled him down into the raft and not a second too soon.

With a gigantic sucking sound the whole stern hoisted high above the water and hung poised like the axe of doom above them. At that moment the poised stern gave a shudder and with the speed of a hammer blow it toppled. As the crew members were trying to swim clear of the ship one lifeboat floated free from the ship. Of the number of men that were dumped into the sea by the sinking Alcoa Partner, twenty-four of them managed to get to this one lifeboat.

The mates that made it to the lifeboat stayed in the area until way after dawn searching for eleven of their missing crew mates. Not finding any of those crewmen they made their way toward

Bonaire and arrived on April 27th thirty- seven hours after the attack on the Alcoa Partner.

Bonaire was about eighty miles from where their ship went down. When they floated into shore the native people helped them with water, food and first aid.

By the next day all the men were on a plane headed back to the United States. The plane windows were covered with black material to darken the interior of the plane. The darkness was more conducive to sleeping and the men were exhausted and nervous.

Joe worked ashore due to nervousness and combat fatigue. After work the drinking continued, until he ended up in the Marine Ward of the Hospital in pretty bad shape. It was the usual ten day stay to dealcoholize the sailor. They gave Joe vitamin injections and general treatment aimed at physical rehabilitation so as to prepare him to be ready to ship out again.

Pauline contacted Joe and asked that they, please, try again to put a life together. She suggested that Joe go to her parent's home in Buffalo, N.Y. He could get a job there with Bell Aircraft. Something new and different sounded good to Joe. Joe left N.Y.C. and lived at Pauline's parent's home. They were very good to Joe and he did get a job at Bell Aircraft. Joe had stopped drinking. He was sober and seemed content to be working at the Aircraft Company. Pauline finished her work as a shipping clerk and moved to Buffalo in late August. Pauline wasn't in Buffalo but a week, they had a fight and Joe moved out. She apologized and they found an apartment together. By November 1942 things were just not working out. Joe felt he had tried and tried again only to have another big fight with Pauline. He wasn't living like this. He headed back to New York City.

The war was going on all around him. Joe wanted to go back to sea. His mother felt that being out to sea triggered more drinking and he had stayed sober for almost five months now.

In a letter Joe wrote to his mother he said,

"Mother, I am afraid you are trying to keep me ashore. When the country that gave you and your sisters and a million others such happiness is fighting, I am going into that battle. I think I am a weakling and the world is full of them kind of people. Remember this is only a testing ground for us all. So I think I should do all I can. If I should not come back, remember you had a son who did what he thought best. I have been a weakling and really don't deserve all the happiness I have had the last five months. I will do more than my share and fight as I live with spirit in it. Fear is something the Lord never wanted us to have. Love and comradeship is good in this world of so many differences.

Your loving son, Joie

P.S. XXXXXXXXX and a billion, billion more.

Thanks for all.

When I come back I'll be a man you can say you are proud of. Everyone else will."

Before he left Joe also wrote his last requests on a piece of paper. The last one read:

"And all the rest will go to my very good mother, who took care of me when my loving wife did not have the sense to do so. I wish that my mother have everything that is mine."

While waiting for his ship and thinking he was in really good shape, Joe had a drink. That was a mistake. In less than a month he was in and out of jail three times for getting into fights, had his front teeth knocked out and owed a hundred dollars to the dentist for fixing his teeth.

Soon after, Joe made up his mind to quit the crap and get his seafarers license. All the younger guys were getting ahead of him and he didn't like it. He felt he had a lot more experience and knowledge than the new comers. Joe went to Fort Trumbull in Connecticut to get his seafarers license. He had made up his mind not to drink for the four months he was there. After three and a half months he was doing so well, he decided a little drink wouldn't hurt. The schooling was all but over. Fort Trumbull's pregraduation dance gave Joe the perfect opportunity to" let loose". Once he started drinking he couldn't stop drinking. He wanted to drink the town dry.

The real clincher came when Joe showed up at the morning exercises in the wrong dress attire. The Lieutenant told Joe to go change and in Joe's mixed up mind he thought the Lieutenant was getting pretty bossy. Joe told the Lieutenant, "You go to hell." You can be sure Joe's exit was quick. He never finished school. He never graduated.

Upon his arrival back in New York City he decided to sit for his seafarers' license there but his nerves were playing tricks on him. The next surprise came when he tried to ship out and was not fit. Joe was sent to Oyster Bay Rest Center. After spending a few wonderful relaxful weeks there getting himself in shape he decided to sit for his license one more time. Again, a few drinks got in his way.

Luckily, he got a job as the Third Assistant with his junior endorsement aboard the S.S. William T. Coleman. The ship was headed to England. He knew he'd better watch himself and the trip went just fine. Upon arriving back here in the states and being paid Joe went out with the guys. Drinking a little too much he tried to slap the chief officer around while out with the crew. He had Joe thrown in jail.

Joe started to realize he had a drinking problem but with a war going on he just kept drinking. He felt he'd probably get blown up by another torpedo sooner or later.

While out drinking one night, Joe got himself in a fight and ended up going through a plate glass window. He woke up the next morning in the Bellevue Hospital prison ward and then the Tombs. The Tombs prison was for the worst offenders in New York City.

He tried to stop drinking again. Joe went out on ship and was doing well, but getting off ship he started that dam drinking. He was back in New York drunk and soon broke. His family and friends were disgusted and sick of his shenanigans.

Joe just kept drinking and was lucky again in getting a ship to take him. He did his work and managed to stay away from the officers on ship. Four or five days before arriving in New York the steward had some drink he wanted to share. Joe wound up stinko again. He was logged for missing watch at sea in the war zone. Joe was drunk when the ship docked and continued that way for a week. He was as sick as a dog and broke.

Joe was fortunate that one of the chaplains at theSeamen's Church Institute recognized the condition he was in and knew how and cared enough about the men to get him to Sands Point Rehab Center in upper New York State.

The Seaman's Church Institute was located right down on the docks. The chaplain's work was to care for the men that made their living out to sea. The church had rooms available for the sailors when they came off the ships and had nowhere else to go, they gave support for mental and physical health, they'd deliver mail to the sailors, had legal advice for those who needed it and help in emergency situations. The chaplains would schedule religious services for the men and women that worked on the docks or on the ships.

It was at Sands Point Joe met Dr. Robert G. Heath. Dr. Heath explained to Joe the situation he was in and what alcoholism meant in Joe's case. He was an alcoholic. If he had even one drink he was on that path to being a no good drunk. He can't drink, period. If he wanted any peace and success in life he must never have alcohol. Alcohol is similar to a poison in Joe's body. Joe listened to Dr. Heath's diagnosis and took it to heart. He did want peace and success in his life.

Dr. Heath recommended Joe go to the A.A. (Alcoholics Anonymous) Club that had formed just two years ago in New York. It was only the second club in the U.S., at the time, started by Bill Wilson, also a recovering alcoholic, and was offering hope to many with the disease of alcoholism. Dr. Heath challenged Joe to get involved and help get the club off the ground. It was struggling.

A.A. Seamen's Club

334 ½ West 24th Street, New York 11, N.Y.

CHAPTER FIVE
Easy does It

When Joe first went to the Alcoholic Anonymous club in September 1944, it was struggling, as Dr. Heath had said. Joe knew hanging around there was not the thing for him to do.

Joe decided to go down to the hospitals and visited with the other Merchant Mariners having the same problems he was having due to alcoholism. He found he understood these men, and he could help them. He visited with them, really listened to them, wrote letters for them, ran errands for them, and visited with their families when asked.

Joe would stop in at the club to see if there was anything going on, or something he could do. Joe started fixing up the club in his spare time, and pretty soon he had other seamen he knew coming in to help him. The club was looking real good. The guys were having a good time together, and they were staying away from the alcohol. Joe brought so many seamen into the club it soon evolved into the A.A. Seaman's Club. They followed all the by-laws of the A.A. Organization, and the twelve steps of Alcoholics Anonymous was their guide, and other men beside seamen were invited in. Just as it takes an alcoholic to understand another alcoholic; it takes a seaman to understand the life of another seaman.

It wasn't long before Joe's efforts started to change things. Eventually, he took over running the club and was paid $17.50 per week for his work. After the first year, Joe's subsistence was raised to $35.00 per week. He knew he'd make more money if he'd go back to the docks and ship out but he also knew his life was changing in positive ways and he was having an impact on others. When you put your interest into helping someone else you begin to realize the mixed up way things were when you think only of yourself. Joe gained a complete release from alcohol. His mind was clear, his thinking straight, and drink meant nothing to him. The drink did not hang over his head as a dread. Every night he'd thank the Lord for guiding him to something that made him see things in a clear light. There's hope if you have faith.

His ability to cooperate, analyze, evaluate and put ideas into motion made the A.A. Seaman's Club approximately seventy-percent a self-supporting organization. Joe told the men, "we owe a great deal to A.A., for without their help we would not exist, and our way of repaying them is to be a constructive part of the organization. A.A. principles state that to properly rehabilitate the alcoholic, he must be shown how to face reality and to be self-reliant. To do otherwise is to fail."

With the help of medical doctors, psychiatric doctors, legal advisors and spiritual advisors, Joe brought to the whole of the maritime field knowledge of the problem of alcoholism among seamen, so that it was effectively dealt with as never before. He got the word out about alcoholism by having talks at the hospitals, weekly meetings at the club, personally contacting the owners of the many different ships, writing articles, word of mouth, his example and personal contacts with hundreds of seamen who had this problem. Derelicts and drunks became sober, reliable, dependable active seamen- licensed and unlicensed. Joe developed an alcoholic project at the Marine Hospital on Ellis Island by working with the doctors and social workers. He worked with patients individually and in groups. Joe gave weekly educational talks on alcoholism. He'd average seeing one hundred twenty-five patients a month in the Marine Hospital.

Joe became the manager and an administrative person for the Seaman's Club. The guys pitched in and helped him carry out an effective program for operating the club. They had business meetings, educational meetings, policy meetings, and social gatherings at the club. Everyone was welcome, but no one, who had been drinking, was allowed to stay if they came in. They were politely asked to leave.

God grant me the *Serenity* to accept the things, I cannot change The *Courage* to change the things I can and *Wisdom* to know the difference.

The Twelve Steps

1. We admitted we were powerless over alcohol—that our lives had become unmanageable.

2. Came to believe that a Power greater than ourselves could restore us to sanity.

3. Made a decision to turn our will and our lives over to the care of God as we understood Him.

4. Made a searching and fearless moral inventory of ourselves.

5. Admitted to God, to ourselves, and to another human being the exact nature of our wrongs.

6. Were entirely ready to have God remove all these defects of character.

7. Humbly asked Him to remove our shortcomings.

8. Made a list of all persons we had harmed, and became willing to make amends to them all.

9. Made direct amends to such people wherever possible, except when to do so would injure them or others.

10. Continued to take personal inventory, and when we were wrong, promptly admitted it.

11. Sought through prayer and meditation to improve our conscious contact with God as we understood Him, praying only for knowledge of His will for us and the power to carry that out.

12. Having had a spiritual awakening as the result of these steps, we tried to carry this message to alcoholics, and to practice these principles in all our affairs.

WOODSTOCK COLLEGE
WOODSTOCK, MARYLAND

Mr. Joseph I. Flynn,
Seamen's A.A.,
New York City.

February 28, 1943.

Dear Joe:

In the current number of the Alumni Bulletin, I noticed an account of your zealous endeavors in behalf of the Seamen. I want to commend you for this work and express the hope that you succeed still more in helping these men. Someday I hope to get to New York and I do hope that I shall succeed in contacting you this time. I shall call up before I come to make sure you are to be there.

By the way, Joe, if you have a reprint of your article in the Quarterly, I would be glad to have one. The young priests here are very much interested in the work and I like to be of assistance to them as far as I can. Several of them have a chaplaincy at the Marine Hospital, Baltimore, and they are very anxious to have the right answers. So that anything that you can send to me will be of use. Incidentally, I have told the young priests to have these boys, when they are in New York, drop in at the Seamen's A.A. I hope you don't mind?

With all good wishes and invoking God's blessing on your work, I am

Sincerely in our Lord,

Hugh J. Bihler, S.J.

Joe kept track of donations, the budget, supplies and maintenance of the building. He formed a mailing list and sent letters or bulletins out to doctors, shipping companies and organizations that might donate money to help the cause. Joe wrote about 700 letters a year. The Seaman's Church Institute which was located right down on the docks was a steady support to the club. Thirty-five hundred people attended meetings at the club in 1947. Joe liked to bring in doctors or speakers to talk to the men. Dr. Heath from Sands Point Rest Center came to the club to talk to the men. Joe, himself acted in direct contact with the men as a lay therapist and counselor. He was a friend to so many alcoholics because he understood them so well. He was once one himself. It became part of his therapy to help others.

He liked to write articles about alcoholism in the pamphlet "For Seaman Who Drink" and over the years he distributed 20,000 copies of the pamphlet. He received a write up in Newsweek in 1945, and in The New York World Telegram, in 1945 and in 1947. His work was so successful that it was written up in the Yale University Journal of Applied Physiology.

While Joe was working at the A.A. Seaman's Club he took the high school equivalency test and passed. He went to night school and took many college courses, earning his associate degree. In the summer of 1946, he received a scholarship to Yale University for a course in their school of Alcoholic Studies.

Joe worked hard to better himself and educate himself so he could help others. The hard work paid off. Joe became a better person, and the club grew under his leadership. He formed lasting friendships with people he met at the club.

Joe took care of other loose ends in his life while at the club. He and Pauline signed divorce papers in 1946, almost four years since he had last seen her, and she had moved on with her life.

He wrote to the United States Maritime Commission and asked for a Certificate of Substantially Continuous Service. He stated that although he didn't go back to the ships after Sand's Point Rest Center, he had been working with the seamen and the ship owners for the last three years. He has helped put together a very successful program for the alcoholic seaman in New York, and its being modeled in other port cities in the United States. Bill Wilson, founder of the A.A. Clubs, also wrote a letter to the Maritime Commission stating all the good Joe's hard work had accomplished, and all the men he had helped. He was granted a Certificate of Continuous Service and honorably released from the Merchant Marines.

From the War Shipping Administration, Joe received The Merchant Marine Defense Bar. This Defense Bar indicated Joe was in active service as a United States Merchant Marine during the National Emergency—September 8, 1939 to December 7, 1941. He was also awarded The Merchant Marine Combat Bar, and The Atlantic War Zone Bar, confirming he was on active duty on a Merchant Ship which was engaged in direct enemy action, and that he was in active service with The United States Merchant Marines in a war area.

With a lot of help and ideas from some of the guys, Joe helped organize talent shows, fun nights, bingo nights, plays and sing-alongs to help raise money to keep the club growing. These events were advertised and open to the public.

A play would take a good six months or more to get ready for. They would have a person who could direct plays come in and help the guys get ready. They would have some of the wives come in to do female parts if needed. The plays were always a big hit.

On Comedy nights or fun nights, the guys would perform routines they had practiced. Joe would team up withhis friend, Jack Crawford, and do a comedy routine as Dr. Fly and Dr. Crow.

One night, Joe did a singing routine. During the singing routine one of the other men acted as an usher and ran up and down the aisles passing out cotton balls for the audience's ears. His singing was enthusiastic but a little off-key. They called him "razor tone baritone". The cotton balls got the audience laughing. Everyone enjoyed the comedy night performances.

It was at one of the fun nights that Joe met Nevada Hoag. Nevada was a student at Mount Sinai Hospital School for Nursing. She had come over to the club with a group of girls for a night out. Nevada could sing and she could play the piano. She did both very well. Joe was taken with Nevada from the first time he laid eyes on her. Nevada was a country girl and a bit reserved but very much taken with Joe. The girls came to quite a few of the fun nights at the club and Nevada and Joe really had a great time together each time she came. They would talk, dance and enjoy themselves so much. It wasn't long before Joe couldn't think of his life without Nevada. Though he proposed in person Joe liked to write his thoughts down on paper.

The ring, he speaks of in the letter, was one he had made with an alexandrite he had picked up when he was in Zanzibar, Africa, as a Merchant Marine. An alexandrite is a greenish-yellow stone that changes color, and appears red in artificial light. Joe was always attracted to things out of the ordinary.

Nevada:

With this ring I humable ask you to become my wife, to share with me all that I have or here fore will be in possion of. wither it be honor, fortune. sickness, health happiness or sadness.

And I promise to care for you. love you, honor you, until death comes and parts us for a short time until we are again reunited where God chossies us to be.

As you become aquinted with this ring it will insterest you, for as the rays of light hit it so it shall change its colors

And as you know me so too shall I change and reviel my self to you, but no matter what color the ring may be its previousness remaines the same. So be it with me for what changes there be in me for bad or good I am yours and of you.

May this ring always act as a symbole of True value and a reminder to you that weither things go good and to our satifation on if they be not good and unsatifieding basicly our love is always the true value, to work for fight for, and live for.

Will you become my wife.   Jodi

Joe proposed in July, Nevada accepted and started making plans for an October wedding. She wrote to her parents, who were out in California, to tell them of her plans. Nevada's parents weren't from California, they were staying out there for a while, panning for gold but would make the necessary arrangements to move back home to Edinburg, N.Y., which is located in the Adirondack mountains north of New York City.

Glenn and Agnes, Nevada's parents were independent living country folks. They did for themselves —sewed most of their clothes, did masonry, carpentry, plumbing, and farming of crops. They had a garden and canned their produce. They did their own butchering, hunting and fishing— or they did without. The biggest problem Agnes could see with this idea of marriage was that Joe was a city man. She wrote in a letter to Nevada that she did not want Nevada to settle down in N.Y.C. "It is no places for a human being to live, exist maybe, but not live. It is the number one target for the next atom bomb that's dropped. Surely, you don't intend to bring my grandchildren up there?" Agnes also had concerns about the fact that Joe lived with his mother, and he didn't have a driver's license. She ended her letter by writing, "Does Mr. Joe Flynn realize how lucky he is to get such a talented, capable, and well educated gal. If he has as much to offer there's no limit to what you can do together. Please, use your head as well as your heart in this business of choosing your husband and the father of your kids."

In the few months before the wedding, Nevada calmed all her mother's fears. Yes, Joe lived with his mother so as to help her with the rent while he was single. He spent so much time at the club, he was never home much. His mother was a very independent lady. He didn't drive because he never had to. He used public transportation and they were going to stay in the city for a while because they both had jobs there.

Joe and Nevada were married on October 25, 1947, at St. Jean's Catholic Church in New York City. They honeymooned at Lake George, N.Y. They even went swimming in October, in Lake George, a beautiful glacier lake with blue, blue water. What a wonderful time they had!

Nevada worked as a nurse at Mount Sinai Hospital and Joe kept working at the A.A. Club. They found a nice little apartment in the city. Joe's mother would fix chicken dinner on Sunday, and they would get together. Sometimes, all three of them would take a train up to Fonda, and meet Nevada's parents for Sunday dinner at the farm.

Nevada left work in June, 1948, and their first child, Winifred Agnes, was born on August 16, 1948. They were so happy and so much in love.

The time came when Joe decided he had to leave the club for other opportunities. He was hired by the United States Department of Commerce to help with the Census of 1948 in the New York Wall Street area. Joe worked nights at the Stork Club, the Commodore Hotel, and the Olympic Club in the Catskills as a bartender. He claimed he was the only sober Irish bartender around!

One of Joe's last letters while at the club was to Dr. Robert Heath, the doctor, who first got Joe to understand alcoholism and what alcohol was doing to his body, mind and, consequently, his life.

Dr. Robert G. Heath
200 Hudson Terrace
Yonkers, N. Y.

Dear Doctor:

Well the time has arrived where that two week job you gave me has come to an end. Little did I know then that those two weeks would amount up to four and a half years.

Sands Point seems a long time ago. The Alcoholic Seamen's Club on 36th Street is now a dream that has faded into all that you ever thought it may become.

Thousands of Seamen have contacted A.A., with many hundreds gaining sobriety and setting an example for other alcoholic seamen to follow. Today the seaman does not feel himself different to the degree that A.A. won't work for him, for now there are many in shore side groups and even prefer these groups rather than their own, making it unnecessary to have a group for seamen alone.

Our Club has changed its name to the Helsmen Club, the membership although in the most part seamen is now made up in a large part of people ashore, which has a good effect on the seamen, giving them the social life they were unable to find before. A Club Committee has taken over the management and for the past six months have been operating effectively. We are just an A.A. Club now, carrying out the regular duties of a group, holding meetings, doint 12 Step work, having social affairs, etc. But most important we are 100% self-supporting, that is without paying me my salary, which has been taken care of by the policy board in the past two years. It is not only for this reason that my job is finished, but for the factor that any future advancement is very improbable, A.A. being what it is, a group where the alcoholic is allowed to give vent to all his inhibitions and peculiarities, and in so doing gains insight into his own actions, whereby he corrects his idiosyncrasies, so that he may fit into the ideal of the group inspiration. To interfere with the process in any way would not allow A.A. to be successful therapeutic means it now is.

Secondly I as an individual belong in society - a living vital part of it, taking all the ups and downs, and making a decent livelihood for myself and my family. This I look forward to, for I feel that I have prepared myself for the life I escaped from at one time.

To go back I can say that I took the job as caretaker, not because I wanted to, but because you were a nice guy who lended encouragement, so I was to stay for two weeks as a favor. O, what an awakening I received since. How little of life I knew, and so much less of myself. And the chance to live was given to me, and the hundreds of others like myself, because you were the kind of person who believed in man with your heart and mind and gave us the chance.

You are not known to the many here now. Your name is mentioned at times among the older members, and you are asked about more out of curiosity than feeling, which is the way of all things.

Personally I am grateful to you and proud to have known you, and to be able to carry out the work you started, and in turn pass on the good that I now feel I have gained. I remain

      Gratefully,

      Joseph I. Flynn

Joe was lining up committees and training new people to take over as he was preparing to leave the A.A. Seaman's Club after four and a half years. He had worked so hard for the men, the club, and accomplished so much educating people about alcoholism it was bitter sweet to move on. Joe had really grown as an individual and discovered what life could be without alcohol. As Joe puts it, "The only difference between as I am now – healthy and contented with dough in my pocket, and nothing too bad to face on my conscience; and some shipmate shaking to pieces with a hangover, broke, and with a grudge against the world – the only difference is one drink."

In October 1949, Joe and Nevada welcomed their first son, Glenn J. Flynn, into the world. Things were getting very cramped in their small apartment, and Nevada was yearning to get back to the country. Joe and Nevada decided to leave the city. The "city boy" was going to the country with his family. They were headed to the Adirondack Mountains with a lot of love, a ton of optimism and a pocket full of dreams.

Joe working for the Department of Commerce Bureau of the Census 1948

Joe graduates from Adirondack College

Joe makes a stop on his Curtis Candy Route

CHAPTER SIX
A New World Opening Up

Joe and Nevada found ground floor cold water flat on Extension of East State Street in Gloversville, N.Y. Nevada would heat up water for the children to take baths or when Joe was home, he and Glenn would head down to the YMCA to get a shower. They had second hand furniture that Nevada would make slip covers for if need be. Nevada would get crates from the grocery store, clean them up or paint them if they were stained. She would stack them to store the kid's clothes in. Nevada was very frugal and knew how to stretch a buck. She sewed the kid's clothes, canned from the garden, baked bread and made thrifty, delicious and nutritious meals. Their third child, a healthy little daughter, Sandra Jean, was born on June 2, 1951.

Joe learned to drive and got his driver's license once he moved to the country. There was a small candy company in Gloversville looking for a salesman. He was hired on as a route driver for the Curtiss Candy Company and given a company truck to drive. He was given a certain route and told to develop it. He introduced many new lines and opened up over 250 new accounts. Joe built up sales so much that he was offered the position of supervisor after only two years. Joe liked the job, and he was doing well but he was restless, he wanted more. He just felt he couldn't do any more for the candy company.

One day while picking up groceries on the way home from work he was talking with the cashier about finding a larger company to work for. The cashier was telling Joe about Albany Frosted Foods. It was the oldest frozen food distributor in the world in the 1950s, and they were looking for sales personnel. Much bigger company has more opportunities, Joe thought.

Joe looked into the company and applied. He was hired on as a route man but with a larger territory than the candy company gave him. Curtiss Candy Company didn't want to see Joe move on, but it was clear he had more ambition than they had a job for.

Joe and Nevada had their fourth child, a delightful baby girl, Joanne, was born on December 18, 1952. They bought their first home on West Fulton Street just outside of Gloversville. It had so much more room, and the neighbors were wonderful. Weekends were always fun and busy. Of course, what isn't busy with four lively kids?

Joe went to auctioneer school and did that on the weekends to earn extra money. He really enjoyed being an auctioneer, he enjoyed being out with people, he liked to hear himself talk, and Nevada would take the kids over to the auction when one was close to home.

Sunday was church day. The whole family would go to church together. Joe was in the Knights of Columbus Organization of the Catholic Church. Once a year they would have a big picnic. There were games and all the food and watermelon you could eat. It was a great time.

Going to Nevada's parent's farm was another great Sunday activity with the kids. Their grandfather was called Glenn Daddy and their grandmother, Bram Bram. Winifred, the oldest, had trouble pronouncing her "G" for Grandmother when she first started talking. They sounded more like a "B". It stuck with her, and the other kids followed suit. Bram Bram it was.

The kids all loved running around outside through the pastures down the "Singing Road." Joe called the path thru the pasture down to the spring the "Singing Road" because it was so relaxing for him to be out for a walk with the kids., He'd start singing as he walked. Usually, the song was "The Big Rock Candy Mountain", only he'd change the words a bit. He'd give all the kids a place in the Big Rock Candy Mountain song. Winifred would be climbing the gum drop trees, Glenn would be at the lemonade spring, Sandra would be in the licorice cart and little Joanne would be listening to the blue bird sing. Life was so good for all of us.

PUBLIC AUCTION SALE

Will sell at Public Auction the entire household effects of, Edith VanLoan, at Pawling Street, next to Grange Hall in the Village of Hagaman, New York.

Sat. Feb. 19, 1955

Commencing at 1:00 P.M. The Following Property :

1. Electric Vacuum Cleaner with Attachment,   Several Scatter Rugs
1. Estate Heatrola, Coal, Large Size,   1. 3 Piece Living Room Suite
1. Dining Table and 6 Chairs,   1. Drop Leaf Kitchen Table
1. New Ideal Sewing Machine, with Attachment,   3. 9x12 Rugs
1. G. E. Electric Refrigerator, 5 feet size,   1. Dresser with Mirror
1. White Enamel Kitchen Range, Oil Burning, Nearly New
1. Writing Desk and Bookcase Combination,   2. Comodes
1. Edison Home Phonogragh with Cylinder Records,   Quantity of household Linens, Dishes, Cooking Utensils etc.   Trunks, Suitcases, Rocking Chairs, & odd Chairs, Plant Stands, Flower Pots, Table and Floor Lamps, Antiques, Dishes, Pictures, Mirrors etc.

Many, Many other Items to numerous to mention

TERMS : CASH and CARRY

The Above Premises Will Be Open From 8:00 A. M. To Auction Time For Your Inspection of Merchandise And Pre-Auction Bid

Administrator,   Your Auctioneer,
F. BANTA   "Congenial" **JOE L. FLYNN**

AUCTION   -   AUCTION   -   AUCTION

Exploring the barn was another fun activity. Just the smell of inside the barn was so special. There is nothing in the suburbs that smells like that. The hay, the horses, the manure, the leather harnesses hanging on the wall, and the wood, all together have a smell only a country kid knows. The rule was you had to wait to go in the barn with Bram Bram for safety reasons. Then again none of us kids were tall enough to get the barn door latch on our own.

The kids liked when Joe's mother would come up to Fonda on the train. Their grandmother on their father's side, they called Nana. Joe would take all the kids down to the train station to meet her. He'd set the little kids on the baggage carts so they could see the train coming in.

Little Valerie was born on June 7, 1954 and John Joseph was born on December 20, 1955. The family was growing and Nevada took care of the kids and things at home while Joe was out earning the money.

Joe was with Albany Frosted Foods almost three and a half years when he earned a promotion due to hard work, imaginative selling and his exceptional organizational skills. In 1957 he was asked if he'd like to transfer to the Frosted Foods Sales Corp. in Syracuse, N.Y., for which Albany Frosted Foods was the parent company, as the sales manager. Joe and Nevada talked this offer over. It would be a huge undertaking moving their young family but they felt it was an opportunity they couldn't turn down. Joe thrived on a challenge. Joe would be in charge of writing and producing all sales material, handling public relations, pricing merchandise, and training the salesmen. He would be in charge of both institutional and retail customers. He felt he was ready for this promotion, and ready to take on a job with more responsibility. Nevada was a realist. She never took life for granted but lived it fully as it came to her. She felt this was a positive move for her family and that's what mattered most in her life.

Joe went ahead to Syracuse to start his new position and find a house. He went back home on the weekends to see Nevada, and the children, and help get everything packed up to relocate. Joe had a couple houses lined up for Nevada to look at and they decided on a cape cod in the village of North Syracuse selling for $10,000. It was located in a nice neighborhood where there were other children for the kids to make friends. They could ride their bikes up and down the street and play in the yards. The elementary school path was only two blocks away. The kids could walk to school, and they held summer school classes, craft classes, music classes, ping pong competitions, dance classes, and plays during the summer for the children. The church, the dentist, the doctors, the library, and the stores were all within walking distance. It was perfect for a young family.

Joe enjoyed the challenges of his new job, learning a new territory and meeting new people. He joined the Food Service Executives Association and was asked to handle their public relations. He also joined the Sales Executive Club of Syracuse. These organizations were made up of salesmen from all over New York State. It was a way for Joe to network with fellow salesmen.

Joe helped start the first food shows in Syracuse. They were great events where all the big food companies would get together and display their products. Restaurant owners, health care supervisors in charge of food purchase, school personnel, and others would all come to sample new food products, and get in on the special pricing for the food show attendees.

Joe had a great sense of humor and would always have gimmicks at his booth. One of his first gimmicks was a can of dehydrated water and a set of wind up chattering teeth. He had a rubber chicken that you couldn't help but notice. Anything Joe could do to get someone's attention, and get them talking about his food booth with others; was exactly what Joe wanted to accomplish. Joe thought, if they are talking about us, they are thinking about our products, and soon or later that means sales.

He was written up in a National Frozen Food magazine for unique endeavors in presenting institutional buyers with the latest products. He challenged the salesmen, he was training, to just get the customer talking about you and your products. These salesmen won wide recognition in all inter-company contests with Joe's coaching.

We didn't always appreciate Dad's jokes because kids don't always understand adult humor or just what a joke is; you learn that as you experience life. When I was in third grade, Sister Gerard was my teacher, and she was teaching us about dehydration. I politely raised my hand, and told her there was a can of dehydrated water that sits on the shelf above our stove. She walked toward me, and told me that was not possible. I started to get upset because she didn't believe me, and I knew I saw that can of dehydrated water. Then she told me there was no such thing, "You can't dehydrate water". I said," But the can is real, I saw it". Not wanting to upset me any further, she asked me to bring it in.

When I arrived home from school that day, I put a stool up next to the stove and climbed up to get that can. .Mom came into the kitchen, "Sandra, what are you doing?" So, I explained what happened at school, and told her I needed to prove to the teacher, I knew what I was talking about. Mom told me, "It's one of your father's jokes". "Mom, I don't care if it's Dad's joke, it's a can of dehydrated water and I told the teacher we had it"! Mom said," Sandra, you can take it to school but it's not really a can of dehydrated water". "Mom, that can says dehydrated water; SEE!" At home, Joe liked to have meetings just like at work. He was always big on getting people together to share ideas. He'd get the kids together in the play room downstairs, Nevada too. He taught the kids to sing this song before and after the meetings.

//We are the frisky, frisky Flynns. We work together, play together, pray together, stay together. We are the frisky, frisky Flynns.//

Chores were discussed, along with situations we had, or opportunities that were coming our way. Everyone, who wanted one, was given a turn to talk. Nevada wasn't a big talker like Joe was. She was very straight forward, direct and logical. Nevada would say , "I mean what I say and say what I mean,". Of course, she didn't have much time for discussion, there were always dishes to do, clothes or diapers to fold, kids to get to bed and preparations for tomorrow.

Joe had a big old crank printing press down in the basement. One rainy Sunday afternoon we were down there with dad picking out all the letters to put in the press to make little cards.

The business cards read:

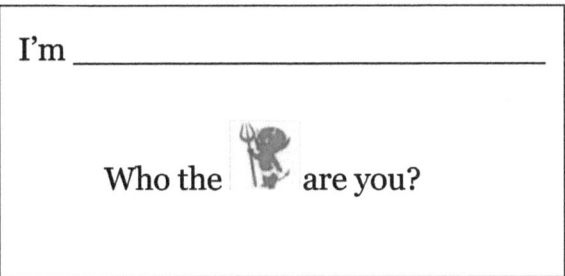

Oh, it was great fun printing them out on a rainy afternoon. The next day Joanne was passing them out at school. We went to a catholic school and one of the nuns caught her with them. The nuns were horrified by such "trash" in school and asked where she got them from. As proud as any kid could be she said, "Dad helped us print them up in the basement on his printing press." For some reason the nuns didn't appreciate these cute little cards nearly as much as we kids did, and they didn't think they were very funny either.

If they only knew what our other rainy day activities were, like learning to gamble with dad as the dealer. He'd shuffle those cards so good. The cards would look like they could walk right up his arm! Other times, he'd get the roulette wheel out and tell the kids in a deep loud voice to, "place your bets". Then he'd give that roulette wheel a big spin. Sometimes, he'd roll those dice with a wicked shake in his big hands, throw them on the table and say, " seven, take eleven, baby gets a new pair of shoes". Joe knew how to have fun.

At the super table, Joe was ready for conversation. He'd ask how your day was, who you met, or talked to, or did you learn anything new today. If no one had an adventure, or new insight on life to share, he usually had something on his mind. It might be something as farfetched as, "What do you think about reincarnation?", or "Does anyone know where I could get some really strong glue? I was thinking we could glue pins onto dimes and sell them." "Who wouldn't want a dime-on-pin?" He loved to hear your thoughts and have conversations.

Joe was traveling the N.Y. State Thruway on the way home from one of his sales trips. It was late and rainy on a Thursday night when he got to the North Syracuse exit. When he opened his wallet he realized he had no money. He reached into his pocket, only a few coins, not enough to pay the toll. So he said to the attendant, "I have this gold watch, will you take this as collateral for my Thruway fare? I will come back tomorrow, and pay you the money I owe you. I'd really like to get home tonight but I'll be back with the money I owe in exchange for my watch back. You can count on it." The toll booth attendant went along with the honest request. Joe returned the next day, paid his toll and received his gold watch back.

Daniel Robert was born on December 13, 1957, and the youngest of the Flynn kids, a baby girl named Christine was born on May 14, 1959. Joe and Nevada had a busy life and a full house. In 1963, they moved to a larger home in North Syracuse. It was a split level in a very nice development but a bit further from town.

The new house had an office in it for Joe, which he really needed and appreciated. He spent hours in his office. The kids were all getting older and friends would call for them at the house. The Flynn family was one of the first families to have two telephone numbers in the telephone book. Under a listing for Flynn, Joseph I. and his telephone number, the directory listed kid's phone GL8-4025. Joe didn't want to miss any calls from his customers when he was home.

Joe was interested in the study of handwriting and joined the Grapho-Analysis Association. Handwriting is not merely a grouping of letters, but rather a grouping of strokes, each of which has an individual value. So much can be deciphered about an individual from their handwriting. As Joe got more proficient in analyzing handwriting he'd have a booth at the church bazaars and talk with people about their handwriting. One or two of the kids would go along to pass out pencils and paper. On a piece of paper, he'd tell the people to write: my t's tell tall tale tales. People would be amazed how he could tell them things about their personalities just from that small sampling of handwriting. Joe served as president of the Grapho - Analysis Association for many years and taught classes in handwriting analysis at the Syracuse YMCA.

Ventriloquism also fascinated Joe. He went to classes and learned the principles of throwing your voice. His dummies were named "Knuckle Head", "Rosie", and "Danny Jr. Jr." Joe would have so much fun with them. He changed Knuckle Head's name to "Money" because "everybody loves money," he said. Nevada made hand held puppets out of socks and felt for Joe. He'd take them to food shows to attract attention and an audience.

Joe's work with Syracuse Frosted Foods was very successful; under his guidance, sales increased from $10,000.00 to $40,000.00 a week, overcoming stiff and aggressive competition, and helping to make Frosted Foods the leading frozen food distributor in Central N.Y. He went to see his manager about working on commission. Salary was alright for some men it served their needs, helped them budget, and gave a secure feeling to their life, but Joe wanted to be paid for what he did. He told the boss," if I don't make any sales you don't owe me a thing but if I'm out making money for this company, and training salesmen to make money for this company, I'd like to be put on commission". Syracuse Frosted Foods never paid salesmen on commission, they paid all salesmen a salary. Joe started looking around for a commission based sales position with greater opportunities.

Joe and classmates in the Bill Davis Class for ventriloquism

In 1962, Joe started selling soup bases for a company out of Chicago, Custom Food Products. Bob Potts, a good friend and mentor, told him about this company and was a big help in getting Joe started. He taught Joe about " follow thru" with customers. Bob would tell Joe, "It isn't until the third or fourth time you call that you make a sale; so make that stop again, talk to that owner again." Bob also taught Joe about contests. "For every three cases of soup base they buy, give them half a case. Give them an incentive to buy from you. You have a good product, push it." Bob helped get Joe off to an excellent start with Custom Foods.

Joe was paid $100.00 weekly to start, plus $100.00 for on the road expenses. He was on the road three or four days out of the week. After six months, he was strictly on commission, just as he wanted things to be. They gave him the New York State area. Joe was good at selling, and making himself available to his customers. He liked selling. He enjoyed the lifestyle of a salesman. He made the most of being on the road. While in the car he'd listen to tapes on sales and marketing, tapes on living life, eliminating self-doubt, how your thoughts can change your life, the power of the mind, and tapes on hope, gratitude, humor and positive thinking. His mind was sharp and always ready to learn.

Joe's father, who was living in California had kept in touch with him through letters. Telephone calls were expensive, so few were made. His father wrote that he was having health problems. Joe offered to help him out if he'd come back east. They made arrangements, and Joe picked up his father at the airport. Joe had already picked up his mom, she was at the house. Well, when Grandpa walked thru the back door with a cane and looking much older than when Nana last saw him, thirty years ago, she went into hysterics! We never saw her laugh and loose it like that. When she calmed down some, she kept saying, "You're a little old man"! "You're a little old man"!

Grandpa never missed a beat, he said to her, "You been drinking again?" Nana was vain and very unaware of her own aging, though she too, had aged quite a lot in the thirty years he was gone.

Joe had moved his mother to an apartment in Syracuse so she was closer to family Grandpa had a bed in the boys bedroom for a short time when he first came. Joe soon had to find him an apartment in the city. He was a cantankerous old man who liked to smoke in bed or have a nip or two. He had a real smart mouth which made him hard to live with. Every Sunday Joe would pick them both up for dinner. Nana made a point to let Joe know to always pick her up first and on the way home drop her off last. She didn't want the old man to know where she lived. He would call and tell her, he was coming over to her apartment just to get her riled. Why, the old man couldn't drive and he even had trouble walking. It was just his personality to egg her on any way he could and Nana would always fall for his ribbing.

One Sunday at the house Grandpa said to Nana," They named a town after you in Massachusetts". Nana, being Nana, couldn't help but be flattered, "Really, what's the name of the town"? Grandpa replied, "Marblehead"!

Joe was a remarkable man in that he held no malice toward his father. He never judged him harshly, he accepted his father just as he was. Things that had happened when he was a kid and a young man, between he and his dad, or his mom and dad were always kept in the past. Joe did the best he could for his father when he needed help in old age. He got his groceries; picked him up for Sunday dinner every week with the family. Nevada washed his clothes and helped fill out paperwork to get him a caregiver, doctor or medicines. Joe never scolded him for giving Nana grief. It would have been like telling the dog to stop barking or the cow to stop mooing. Grandpa was unconditionally accepted and loved just as he was. The old man was his father and Joe did the best he could for him. Joe felt most people are doing the best they can, and he had a very strong sense of family.

Grandpa died on September 6, 1972. Joe took care of all the funeral arrangements. Grandpa had asked for a mass at the Catholic Church, in his Last Will and Testament that he had written on May 11, 1970. He also asked that his burial plot be recognized by a marker, which was to include his name, date of birth and date of death. They were such simple requests. Joe, Nevada, Nana, and some of the kids who still lived in Syracuse went to the funeral home to say good-bye. Joe was a good speaker and he did an excellent job of remembering his dad.

One advantage of the kids getting older was that Joe could hire them to fill out the spread sheets with the customer's names, what they ordered, and how often they ordered. Joe could keep track of his sales better and remind the customers they were getting low on a product which they often appreciated. It was a way of increasing his sales and helping his customers out. The girls liked working on the spread sheets it gave them a little spending money. Joe would often remind them to "put some in the bank for a rainy day", and "put a dime in your pocket in case you need to call home".

Joe wanted to leave something with his customers and the other salesmen, so he started writing the "SOUP SPOON SCOOP". It was only one page of the latest news in the food industry. Joe would put in sales tips, news about a new product, and articles on how to prepare a product already in the product lineup but maybe not selling as well as it should be. Of course, he'd always have a joke or two. Joe referred to his soup bases as "Cosmetics of the Kitchen" He'd tell the salesmen, "Never, never sell soup bases on price; sell the flavor, the satisfaction, and the fine results from using the right base. What you're really telling them is you want their business to remain good or grow." He'd sign off his articles by writing, "In creative selling," or

Joe, president of Grapho-Analysis Association

"Magical Joe"

"Good Selling", or Joe I. Flynn "The Custom Man". The customers and the salesmen enjoyed reading the latest "SOUP SPOON SCOOP".

In 1965, Joe joined a magic group. He always had an interest in magic but never the chance to find a magic organization before this. He joined the group, and met some fascinating people. He'd get impatient practicing all by himself. He wanted to show someone what he could do. One of the daughters was having a few friends over from her 10th grade class; Joe was going to show them this new trick, he barely knew. He hit a glitch in the trick, and tried to manipulate the ending. Too late, a couple of the young guys caught him, and they didn't let him forget it either. What a blow to a magician's ego. However, it didn't detour Joe, he laughed, took it in stride and eventually picked up the knack of performing some really great tricks. He liked the coin tricks. He was fascinated by money. Every year the magicians would get their families together, have a picnic, play some games, and perform some of their best tricks or illusions. It was always such a fun event. The magician's shows were awesome. Joe was always ready for a show. Everyone had a fabulous time. Joe was a member of both The Society of American Magicians and The International Brotherhood of Magicians.

It was also in 1965, that Joe won the Mr."C" title. Custom Food Products gave this award to the salesman who most increased his sales for the year. Joe really moved the bar to a new standard. He increased his sales by 30.89%. It would be hard to beat that kind of increase in sales in a year.

In 1971,he heard about the Creative Education Foundation conducting the Creative Problem Solving Institute, which was held for two weeks in June at Buffalo University in Buffalo, N.Y. or in San Diego, California. People would come from all over the world. In exchange for teaching their expertise they could attend classes by others who taught their expertise. After Joe's first year he was invited into leadership, and asked to teach a class about selling.

Over the next twenty-six years he attended CPSI every year in June and taught seven different classes: One- The Art of Selling Methods, Skills and Philosophies; Two- We're All Selling Something – Why Not Use Professional Tools; Three-Ideas-How to get Them, Take care of Them and Use Them; Four-You're Number One; Five- Imagination Can Be Fun; Six-Age- a state of mind, and one year taught a class on –Hugs- . Some years he'd teach two classes, and the basic seven classes would have revisions each year to keep them interesting. Joe was sold on creative thinking and brainstorming. During that twenty-six year period that Joe attended the Creative Problem Solving Institute he sponsored his wife, all his children, some of their spouses, and five of the grandchildren.

In 1978, he received the Colleague of the Creative Education Foundation Award; in 1981 he received his Certificate in Creative Studies from Buffalo State University.

In August of 1974, after twelve years with Custom Foods, and an increase in sales over the past three years of 53.6% due to more creativity, the company offered Joe a larger territory. Joe and Nevada talked this offer over. She was behind him all the way. Joe was one of their top salesmen and without hesitation he began selling in Pennsylvania, New Jersey, New York, Maryland and Virginia.

Joe, Nevada, two of the kids, who were still at home, and Joe's mom, Nana, who was living with them, were all moving to Dillsburg, Pennsylvania, located just outside of Harrisburg. It was a more central location in the new sales territory. Joe had just celebrated his 57th birthday but slowing down was not on his list of things to do or even a part of his vocabulary. He was gearing up for a larger sales territory and more opportunities. You could hear him singing in the shower, "Sell, Sell, Sell"

at the food show

At home in the office

Custom Food Products, Inc.
3125 W. CHICAGO AVE. • CHICAGO, ILLINOIS 60622 • AREA CODE 312•722-7520

January 21, 1966

Mr. Joe Flynn
112 Newport Drive
No. Syracuse, New York 13212

Dear Joe:

Congratulations---you are "Mr. C" for the year 1965. You have topped the sales increase of many fine men and come out with the coveted solid Gold watch award. I am most happy to inform you that your sales increase for the year was 30.86%. This is phenominal.

Joe, we are well aware of the fact that it takes concentrated, intelligent hard work to come up with such an increase. We know that you have been putting in this concentrated hard work and offer our sincere congratulations on this excellent achievement. We therefore designate you:

Mr. "C" - 1965

CUSTOM FOOD PRODUCTS, INC.

M. J. Phee
Vice President - Sales

MJP:bt

CHAPTER SEVEN
Living Life to the Fullest

Joe and Nevada found a very nice ranch home situated on a little over an acre just outside of Harrisburg, in the small town of Dillsburg. Their new home was nicely situated out of town, yet the town was close by. There was a room for Joe's office, a sewing room for Nevada, an extra living room in the downstairs, a two car garage upstairs, garage on the lower floor with an extra high ceiling, a cold cellar, a bedroom on the lower floor, and three bedrooms upstairs. The kitchen and living room upstairs were spacious. The house had plenty of room for everyone and great lighting due to the large picture windows. It was practically brand new and sold for $57,500.00. It was August 1974. Joe hired a moving company to do the moving. It took a while but things settled down after a bit, as they always do.

Nana, Joe's mother, was 89. Her health was failing and her mind would wander. Nevada set up a very nice room and kept her on a schedule, since consistency seems to help with older people. She did well at first, but by her 90th birthday, she was mostly bedridden. Her grown grandkids came to visit and keep her company, which she enjoyed so very much. If we were in a hurry and stuck our head in the door to say, "Hi" she'd say, "It doesn't count as a visit unless you sit down".

She was a big influence in our lives growing up. She'd tell us kids, "Don't go out (of the house) by yourself, you could be kidnapped". When we were young, she would send packages from New York with little gifts for all the kids, and always with mothballs. She put mothballs in everything; her drawers, her suitcases and her packages. One time, she sent a big box of chocolate bars with moth balls. We kids were so excited to get candy. Well, you should have tasted those chocolate bars. They tasted like moth balls! We had to throw them all out.

We took turns visiting Nana in New York City with dad. She lived two blocks off Broadway. Every day, she would walk to the fish store or the deli to get something for dinner. She had no freezer space, her refrigerator was tiny and the stove had only two burners, and no oven.

During those years when we'd visit Nana, we'd go to Coney Island, out to eat at the Chinese Restaurant, out to the stores or the movie theater but she warned us, "Don't go across the street to the big apartment building. There were two murders there last week." While Nana told us to run away if a stranger ever tried to grab us, Dad told us, "You know right where to kick him."

Back in 1964, Joe took his mom, who was 79 at the time, to the World's Fair. It was held in New York City. She saw things she never dreamed of as a kid over in Ireland. It was an amazing event. Nana had the time of her life. What a thrill for her.

She liked life in the big city. New York City was home to Nana. Moving to Syracuse was hard on her, though I never really heard her complain. I went to a catholic high school in Syracuse, so after school or on a half day of school I'd go see Nana. She would want to walk downtown, which was only a few blocks from her apartment. On the walk she'd tell me about how there were no big department stores, no deli, and no fish stores in Syracuse, not at all like New York. It just wasn't the same as her beloved New York.

We'd go to the five and dime store, "Woolworths" where they had a lunch bar with swivel stools. Nana would always order a grilled cheese on white bread with a coke. Oh, how she enjoyed that for lunch. If you were shopping with Nana, you had to be careful not to wander out of her sight. She would yell your name so loud, her voice would squeak and the whole store could hear her, and it wasn't only once she yelled!

Nana would give us girls unsolicited advice at times. She'd warn us, "Never let a boy kiss you on the lips, you tell him to kiss you on the cheek." (Germs were the issue) Another time, she told us, "If a boy gives you a ring and you don't want to see him anymore, don't give that ring back, take it to the hock shop, and get money for it." Nana also warned me not to scrub the floors on my knees, "Those knees will bother you when you get old like me. You won't be able to walk".

Nana died in February 1976. Nana never had much as far as possessions go. She never owned a house, a car, a pet or even had a hobby. She never had any new furniture, books, pictures or knickknacks to speak of in her apartment. She lived life on her terms, never asked for much, never needed much and she was always self-reliant. Joe took care of her funeral arrangements, her mass and her burial in Edinburg Cemetery, New York, right next to Grand Pa. Not sure how happy she would be about that! Joe then gave each one of her grandkids a check for five hundred dollars. He divided up her life savings among her nine grandchildren. Savings no one imagined she even had. Nana would have been so proud to be able to give the people she loved such a gift.

Sometime later, Joe wrote in a letter to his brother, Jack, "Once in a while mom and dad run across my mind. I think they were both very successful in their own way; dad with his humor, his guts and persistence; mother for her love, loyalty, kindness, thoughtfulness, caring attitude, and a 1,000 more. God Bless them both."

Joe flourished in his job selling Custom Foods, Soup Bases and Gravies. He was on the road four or five days a week and working from his office at home the rest of the time. The next ten years of his career, his selling techniques were remarkable. He was always coming up with a new sales pitch, a new sales gimmick to get the customers attention or a new promotion. They were the "Million Dollar Sales Award Years" for Joe. He was at the top of his game. He was the top sales executive in the company.

While on the road, Joe would listen to cassette tapes. His time in the car between customers or on the drive home became his classroom. He listened to tapes on selling, marketing, helping the customer build his business or how to get along with people. Joe enjoyed tapes on personal growth, understanding life, physical and mental health, and the power of the mind to eliminate self-doubt, and discover how your thoughts can change your life. He would enjoy messages of hope, forgiveness, gratitude, love, happiness and developing an unshakeable confidence in yourself, in those around you and in the world in general.

The world was changing, and computers were becoming a big part of sales. This was a big learning curve for Joe, who was in his 60's. He was so intrigued by the computer. Joe got his own desktop computer and he spent hours learning how to do the programs. In the early 1980s, you had to pay for long distance phone calls. That didn't stop Joe or even slow him down, he'd call Texas to talk with the experts of the Apple computers when he got in a pinch, or his computer wasn't working just right. He'd be typing on the computer, and occasionally the screen would turn black and in big white letters – THINKING- THINKING- would move across the screen for several minutes and then the screen would return to where he was typing. He found this fascinating and amusing. He did eventually become very good at using the computer. Joe would tell you, "Stick-to-it-iveness" is what you need to achieve at anything."

At home, things were busier than ever. Nevada was the floor nurse at Messiah Village, a nursing home just a mile or so from the house. Two of the kids were living at the house with mom and dad, another was about five miles away and another was only two miles away. Nevada's father and Joe's nephew were also living with them. There was just a lot going on in all their lives.

Nevada's father, Glenn Daddy, was a veteran of World War 1. He had been a butcher and a cattle dealer. He was a strong, quiet, self-sufficient individual who liked to be outdoors working, fishing or hunting. When he was younger, he bought an old farm and rebuilt the house, the garage, and the barn. He made a wonderful home for his family, and built an awesome patio on the side of the house. The patio had a fireplace for cooking, and over the front of the chimney hung the old ox yoke from his team of oxen. A big wagon wheel strung with lights hung on a tree on the side by the picnic table for gatherings at night. He built Adirondack chairs for friends and family to relax in. Glenn Daddy was a solid, wonderful influence on our lives as children. He was 92 now and needed Nevada's help. He had developed dementia, and was getting very weak. Joe admired Nevada's father and would always take time to talk with him when he was home. They had very different backgrounds, and interests but they were both very hard workers. Glenn Daddy lived with Joe and Nevada, for about a year and a half, until he entered into eternal rest on August 30, 1980.

Joe's brother, Jack, who lived in Bogota, South America, sent his son, Robbie, to stay with the Flynn clan for a year. Jack had an alcohol problem and was very impatient with Robbie, who was 17, at the time. Robbie was a very quiet personality, who spoke broken English. Joe became his mentor. Life in America was a much faster pace than Robbie was used to. Life at the Flynn home was very hectic with everyone coming and going. Joe was always willing to try, and help people out. He spent hours talking with Robbie, trying to help him understand his father, and not let his father's idiosyncrasies shape his life in a negative way. Robbie was old enough to take responsibility to choose, and define his own life. Joe told him, he needed to live his life in a way that makes him a better person, and contributes to the good of others. Robbie enrolled in school and looked for a part-time job. He decided to go back home earlier than planned but it was a great experience for everyone concerned.

Joe was having trouble writing on the board at his presentations and he was having weak spells for no apparent reason. The doctor didn't think much of it, he just told Joe that he was getting older. Joe went along with it at first for no other reason than he was not a doctor, and was preoccupied with so many other things in life, but his body kept telling him something was wrong. He was determined to find out what was going on. Joe contacted another doctor, who sent him to a neurologist. The neurologist's diagnosis – Parkinson 's disease.

In Joe's words, "I continued working, holding down a marketing job covering five states for a manufacturer from Chicago, Illinois. I enjoyed success as a territorial sales manager, procuring some of the company's very best accounts. I was with the company for about twenty years at the time, and I was sixty-nine years old, and in very good health except for this new scenario – Parkinson's Disease. My battle with Parkinson's during the first year or so did not come to anything. I took my pills on a regular basis and did my exercises daily. My sense of humor, and positive attitude did not suffer to any degree, my sales remained firm even with changes in the commercial food business. I liked my work and was making more money than ever. Parkinson's made me realize that my days as a super salesman were just about over."

With that being said, Joe did what Joe does, he learned all he could about the disease that was taking over his body, and he started a Trindle Road Parkinson's Support Group in Mechanicsburg. His idea was to invite the best doctors and social workers to come to the group, talk to the people about the disease, coping mechanisms, experiences and maybe find a cure. Joe liked to accomplish things, he was an organizer, he was a meetings man, and he liked to know what others were thinking. For the next eighteen years, he arranged monthly meetings, snacks, and activities or speakers.

Nevada's mother, Bram, came to visit with Joe, Nevada and any of the kids who could come see her. Bram's abdomen was much extended, but she didn't trust doctors. She said, "I'd go to a good veterinarian if I knew one but I'm not going to no doctor." Nevada hoped she would change her mind but respected her wishes and did everything she could to make her comfortable.

Nevada was a lot like her mother in so many ways. They both spoke in riddles, which we never enjoyed as children. Let's say we spent almost all day hemming a dress and it didn't come out even. We'd be so upset, and Mom would say, "Nobody's going to notice from a galloping horse." Or worse yet she would say, "Just rip it out and start over again." When we were older we learned to appreciate and understand those little riddles about life.

When we kids were growing up we'd take turns spending summers at the farm with Bram and Glenn Daddy. Bram always took time to cook delicious healthy meals. She was a self-educated nutritionist, who believed in preventive care, raising your own meat, and growing your own vegetables. No sugar cereals were in her cupboard. Her cookies were even healthy and delicious. She came up with the recipe for "survival cookies" in the days long before healthy snack bars even came out in the health food stores. Bram helped teach us to cook, bake, sew, knit, crochet or tat. She made clothes, hats, mittens, stuffed toys, pillows, and blankets. When the wool pants or coats wore out, she would strip the wool material into one inch strips to make beautiful hooked rugs. Bram was independent and hard working. She always spoke her mind even though you might not want to hear it.

Bram was only with Joe and Nevada five days when she passed quietly in her sleep on March 27, 1987. She was buried next to Glenn Daddy in the Edinburg Cemetery, which was just a couple miles from where their farm was located.

Joe and Nevada took care of all four of their parents when the time came. They both considered this a privilege and wouldn't have wanted it any other way.

Nevada's and Joe's 40th wedding anniversary was coming up, and the thought of taking that once in a lifetime trip was on Joe's mind. Joe knew his health was a big concern. If he was going to do any traveling, he'd best do it now rather than later

He and Nevada had gone to Hawaii back in 1973. Oh, it was a glorious time. They experienced the waterfalls, the black sea beaches, swimming in the ocean, whale watching, and going to a Hawaiian Luau. The food at the luau was out of this world, with a traditional roasted pig, coconut rolls, fresh- caught fish, and rice. They even heard Elvis Presley sing in concert. Nevada, who always thought Elvis had a built in smirk, was blown away when he sang, "Can't Help Falling in Love". She gained a whole new respect for the singer her kids were so hooked on.

When the kids were young and at home there were day trips everyone enjoyed to Cooperstown, Auriesville National Shrine of the North American Martyrs, Corning Glass Works, Story Town, the Burnet Park Pool, or the Zoo at Burnet Park, the beaches on Lake Ontario, Oneida Lake or Green Lake, the farm, and the New York State Fair. After the kids left home, Dad always tried to get everyone together each summer for a reunion. He'd have them at his home, up at Glenn's place near Lake Ontario, J.J.'s place on Lake Oneida, or a state park nearby. The place Joe picked didn't matter as much as getting everyone together.

Now, he thought, it was time for a trip to Alaska. Joe had always wanted to go to Alaska, and what a time they had. Joe described it, "We spent one full week aboard ship stopping at various ports. We did the usual tourist things, but in addition, I petted some sled dogs, panned a little gold (very little), and ate sourdough biscuits with reindeer sausage. The country was beautiful. High, rugged, snowcapped mountains coming right out of the ocean! The scenery was most impressive." It truly was the trip of a lifetime."

Joe's Parkinson's was slowly changing his life. He knew it was time to retire. In 1988, at the age of 71, he left the commercial food business as one of the top sales people for Custom Foods. He was proud of the job he had done, and headed into retirement full of ideas and plans.

His plans included attending the yearly Humor seminar in Saratoga, New York. Joe explained it as, "Three days of pure joy and laughter. I plan on being a jolly old man." He also planned on attending the Creative Problem Solving Institute in Buffalo, N.Y. for the sixteenth year. Of course, he couldn't miss that! That week each year was a super big part of his life.

The way he figured things out, "Above all else I want to endeavor to continue my studies of the human race. I plan on getting smarter as I grow older. There is so much to learn and I am very curious about life. I am also taking more interest in the Christian principles in our society. It seems many have forgotten we're not here to stay."

For Joe, it was a time in life when you were at the end of one journey only to begin another. He planned so many things for this adventure called "retirement".

On the ship to Alaska

At the Humor Institute

CHAPTER EIGHT
A Fading Full Moon

Joe took to retirement like a fish to water. He signed up for a sign language class at the local high school, and joined the Cursillo group at church. He became more active in the Dillsburg Lions Club, the Knights of Columbus, and the American Legion Post #945. He continued to stay very active in the Creative Education Foundation of Buffalo University, the Society of American Magicians, and the International Brotherhood of Magicians. His Parkinson's Support group was meeting every month and he wouldn't miss a meeting with that group. He stopped in at the local Senior Citizen center to get acquainted. There was so much to do at the Senior Citizen Center. Joe had the opportunity to write the newspaper column, Senior Citizen News, in the Dillsburg paper each month. He had so many ideas and life experiences to share and writing was something he really enjoyed doing. The director of the senior center didn't need to ask Joe twice. Joe wrote articles about Parkinson's disease, playing cards, how important saying "Thanks" is, character, authority, exercise, taxes, responsibility, influence, resentment, spiritual maturity, social security, freedom and growth in the U.S.A., death, and so many more topics for the next six years.

Joe taught classes at the Senior Center, much like the ones he taught at the Creative Problem Solving Institute. The other seniors loved these classes, especially the ones on "Age- a state of Mind", and "Imagination Can Be Fun". "Hugs" was the other class that was so well received. Joe always had handouts in the form of buttons and booklets. In the "Hugs" class he even had a license to hug to give to each one in his audience. Oh, it was official, too. The license had each person's identity information, picture and the stamp of The Department of Affection, number and date. The Commissioner of Affection at the time was William

Holdem. On the back, it read "This is to certify that the person named and described on the reverse side has been licensed to help make our planet a nicer place to live on through the power of hugging." Joe made all his classes fun and encouraged everyone to brainstorm and come up with ideas for the next get together or to tell stories of what was going on related to the class in their own lives. He liked to see people laughing and learning.

Joe did volunteer work with the county aging office. They had a friendly visitors program for seniors who had trouble with mobility and were home alone most days. Joe really enjoyed reaching out to these people and sitting and sharing an afternoon with them. He'd share stories about life, or the news around Dillsburg and the world. He often found that though they may be shut-ins now, they had very interesting lives and families, and he enjoyed hearing about all their adventures.

Like any organization the Lions Club needed to raise money for their charitable programs in the community. Joe started a balloon sales program at the Dillsburg Farmer's Fair. It was a big success, and Joe walked the streets selling those big balloons on sticks with another member during the fair. They had a great time with the people and made money for the Lion's Club to continue their programs.

In 1995, Joe and Nevada were crowned the Farmer's Fair Senior King and Queen. Scott Shughart, director of the senior center, spoke before the "transfer of power" occurred. Scott said, "In addition to being active participants in the senior center, Joe and Nevada have donated countless hours of service and volunteer work to the community." They both were given crowns as they sat in those big chairs. They wore those crowns like royalty. It was an awesome moment.

It was around 1996, that Parkinson's was really slowing Joe down. He came home one day, and told Nevada how the bridge started to narrow as he was driving over it.

Another day, he was telling Nevada that the McDonald's sign jumped out in front of his car as he turned in to get a milkshake.

It was extremely hard to give up driving. He had made his living driving to see customers, sometimes in five different states, for the last forty years. He felt he was losing his independence. It was a hard transition. Joe's mind was still very active though his body was failing him. He still had the mindset of going and doing, but he couldn't drive safely anymore. It was time.

Nevada became his principle driver. If one of his grown children were home, they were always glad to drive dad, wherever he needed to go. It wasn't long before he learned that the Senior Citizen Center had a van, and he'd have the van come pick him up almost every day. Joe would go over for lunch, a game of pool, or to just visit. He was a people person and he needed that outlet. Nevada would take him to all his appointments, and one of the men from the Cursillo Group would pick him up for those meetings. Things always had a way of working out.

Joe experienced periods of "freezing", where his feet wouldn't move. Walking became difficult and his speech was very hard to understand. His hands would shake continually. Nevada was his caregiver. Nevada had trouble hearing and Joe had trouble talking. This whole journey became extremely hard on the both of them. Nevada was two years younger than Joe, he being eighty-two and Nevada being eighty, and her being smaller in stature made things very challenging.

One morning, Joe rolled off his bed onto the floor. He laid there. He just didn't know what to do. His voice was weak and his speech was incoherent. Nevada could not hear him if he yelled for help, she was out in the kitchen. In his mind, he's saying to himself, "God helps those that help themselves. I have to do something to help myself, there's no one but me here." Joe began to roll his body in a very cumbersome manner to the door of the bedroom, down the sixteen foot hallway, and into the living room. Nevada finally came out of the kitchen and saw Joe on the floor. She tried to help him get into a chair. She just couldn't pick him up, and he didn't have the coordination to help her. In Nevada's world few situations qualify as emergencies, and she really didn't like to bother people. After a few more unsuccessful attempts, she sat on the floor next to Joe and read him the day's mail and the newspaper. About three hours later, and after another unsuccessful attempt to get Joe into a chair, she decided to call for help. When help arrived, there they were, both sitting on the floor reading.

The muscles in Joe's throat were failing to function properly. When he tried to eat or drink something it would go to his lungs, instead of his stomach, leading to pneumonia. Joe was put on a feeding tube, and he entered the nursing home where Nevada had worked for 17 years. His care was just too much for any one person. Joe was a prisoner in his own failing, frail and shaking body.

The nursing staff at Messiah Village called to let Nevada know that they found a silver dollar in Joe's bed. This was of concern to them, because if Joe lost that silver dollar, or another patient picked them up, the nursing home would be responsible. Joe always carried silver dollars with him to do little magical tricks or to just hold in his hand. We were not about to take them away from him. He has had to give up so much already. Nevada signed another paper that she was aware of Joe having silver dollars, and the nursing home was not responsible in case of loss. Joe kept his coins.

While at the nursing home, Joe would watch what everyone was doing. He learned where the water fountain located. When things were busy, thinking no one is paying attention, he'd wheel himself over to the drinking fountain and try to get a sip of water to wet his whistle. His lips were so dry and his mouth so parched from never having a drink. He wanted a drink so badly, so very badly. He wanted to drink like he always had. The nurses were always not far behind, ready to wheel him back towards his room.

Joe also watched the nurses getting ice cream or jello out of the refrigerator for the other patients. Towards evening when the nurses were busy at the desk writing their reports he'd wheel himself over to the patient's refrigerator to get a little dixie cup of ice cream. How he loved ice cream. The nursing home just couldn't have this, because the family could sue them for Joe's death, if he did manage to get that taste of ice cream he craved. He was on a feeding tube and to have nothing orally.

A meeting was called by the nursing home. All of Joe's immediate family, a couple of nurses, the doctor, and a representative of the nursing home were to be there. Joe was so excited. Meetings were the ultimate experience for Joe, and all his family would be there. What could be more exhilarating?

On the designated day, we all entered this meeting room. The only furniture in the room was a very large cherry table and matching chairs. We all took our places around the table and Joe pulled up in his wheel chair to the head of the table. Things couldn't have been more perfect, in Joe's eyes. The doctor asked Joe what he wanted to eat. In a voice that some couldn't even understand, Joe said," a roast beef sandwich". He wanted to eat like a normal person. The nurses and doctor told us this just couldn't happen, he will die. After forty-five minutes of discussion the doctor told Joe he was allowed a half-teaspoon of water a day. This was not an acceptable solution to his situation. Joe was so put off by the decision he attempted to wheel himself out of the meeting, down the hall, and back to his room never saying a word.

After we all signed the legal papers stating we wouldn't sue the nursing home in the event of death, due to Joe eating or drinking something he shouldn't, we gathered in his room.

Everyone was talking and laughing. Joe was enjoying the company, and he started to relax. This was the way Joe thought about life, full of energy, and a room full his family, was a room full of energy. Joe reached over to his roommate's tray, tightened his hand around his roommate's glass of water and took a big gulp. Now, he was part of the party! All he wanted was a drink of water. He wanted to eat and drink like a normal person. While still alive he wanted to do all he could to keep his life as "normal" as possible. He wasn't afraid of dying. He knew the Lord. He was more afraid of living a life he had no control over, in a sterilized atmosphere, under the constant scrutiny of others. Joe died very peacefully two days later.

Nevada Flynn, left, and Joe Flynn, right, were crowned the 1995 Senior Queen and King for the Dillsburg Farmers' Fair at the Dillsburg Senior Activity Center on Thursday, October 19.

Royalty

A few of Joe's newspaper articles

York County

Dillsburg Senior Center

by Joseph Flynn

Where Is the Crowd?

A popular story told by many retirees is the one about how we ever found time to go to work. There are enough interesting things happening today to keep us busy for many years. Places to go, shows to see, trips to take, books to read, classes to attend on hundreds of subjects. All we need is the interest, the time, a little money, and the health to keep going. We are a go go society.

Twenty or more years ago there were fewer things to do or we just did not get involved in as many projects as ed seem to do today. So we spent more time playing cards and checkers or we were more willing to sit around and chat, exchange ideas, stories, etc. Perhaps we were more interested in belonging to a club. It did seem we needed a headquarters from which to work and a group of people with whom to exchange our stories. Could it be that people listened better in those days or was it because we were more interested in one another and today our interest is in keeping up with the go go society. Where are we going? The cost of food, rent, and running a home now takes two: man and wife working to afford what the man of the house was able to do on his own not too many years back.

It has been observed that there are fewer people visiting senior centers for an entire day, but when the center offers a covered dish supper and some form of entertainment, the whole gang shows up. We all enjoy getting together, bringing one another up to date on what's been going on with us, just being in one another's company is and experience in itself. Let's gibe one another a phone call and meet at the Center: re-established friendships and talk it over. Gee, it's great to be a senior citizen.

The Overall Intelligence

By Joe Flynn

Just how smart can any one of us be? There seems to be no limit to the amount of knowledge. The last figure heard was that man's overall understanding is doubling monthly. In the year of 1800 it was at a rate of doubling every five years. These are only estimated figures. We all know that everything today comes around faster than it did in the past.

There is another thing we can agree upon: There is plenty of knowledge about. We can go back thousands of years in the history of mankind to the ancient civilizations. That's where we learn many reasons for failure. We had philosophers of all ages giving reasons for doing the positive and how to overcome the negative. Many of us have learned and a certain amount of success has been shown over the ages. Some 21 civilizations have built to greatness and went downhill fading out of the picture of today. All there is for us to study to find out what we should do and not do to continue our growth. We are limited even with all our know-how. It seems each generation has to do it on its own. We should be able to use the best of the old and add to it with the best of the new to bring about better results for the good of the whole.

Maybe we're working from the wrong standpoint, starting with the wrong view of things as they should be. Or could it be that the planet earth is just for the purpose of us coming here to learn certain fundamentals? And when the greater number of us learn that bit of knowledge we are able to go to another area and it will be heaven in comparison to what we were able to do in one lifetime here on earth. There is, I am sure, a reason for all that's taking place here. And we all will be pleased to find out. Some of us may have to come back, do it all over again or add to what we should have fully learned. Just a thought.

On The Lighter Side
By Joseph I. Flynn

Thanks

It has been said that if a man is not thankful for his wife, her loyalty, kindness, care for the children, etc., he will not be faithful to her or give her honor. Would not the same thing apply to any of us who do not say thank you, when someone has been nice to us, or did us a favor. Or were we in too much of a hurry to give it consideration. It does seem that we are all better off if we make it a point to day the "thank you" if nothing else, just to do our part. And could not this little matter be an important part in the whole network, how about hello, goodbyes, "how are you today?" to some of us who got in the practice of never saying any extra words for fear of getting into trouble or maybe if you were on the east side of New York, having something hit you in the head or precipitating a fight. So think it over if you have not been giving it a try. The results can be "terrific".

While we're at it have you ever heard when something happens that hurts us. Instead of thinking and saying "just my luck' or "one thing goes wrong everything goes wrong," etc. We should learn to train ourselves to day "what good can I find in this". It could mean we found a way to add good to our time, an new way of doing something that saves time, brings a greater profit, etc.

We all need a plan, a direction in which to go, a goal t obtain, a method of getting what we want. Knowing what we want is the most important factor in preparing ourselves to get it.

Time really goes by fast, so we cannot waste too much time in making decisions; think fast and not half fass.

JAN-97

The Senior Citizen News - April, 1997

On the Lighter Side

by Joseph I. Flynn

Did you ever think as the hearse rolls by that someday you and I will be taking a little trip, never to come back. We all have it in common to be taking the trip.

A write up on the top of the front page of The Patriot News January 15, 1997, noted that the way we cope with death is often undignified. The article summarized the first report on death and dying published over 90 years ago, and indicated that the manner in which we deal with death has not improved any in over 90 years since that survey was taken.

Lamented was the manner in which death is put off, ignored, and not talked about as if it was a side issue in the world we are now a part of. Anything that real and true has a method of hounding us, a pressing matter in our society. We know it's there, but unable to deal with it, we put it off, we don't see it and don't recognize it. When the time comes that we need to face it we are so helpless and fearful.

They say that there are advantages to every disadvantage. I am sure there are a good many, to something that we all have to face. For as soon as we're born the possibility of dying is a very important part of life. Yet most of us live as if there is no ending. How better it would be if we made dying a vital part of living, and plan on our going away trip. It can be a wonderful event, a well earned reward, which it is. No wonder many of us really only exist and are not fully alive. I for one would like to hear more about dying. I feel very much that such knowledge would be a help in my living a more full life, for one should strive toward getting a broader view of what life is all about. Thereby, we would learn to enjoy life as a whole.

To live is to fully appreciate the nature of the greater power, to be fully awake with knowledge of self and understanding of others. This world is but a check-in operation where we find out what we would like to do in the next.

Enthusiasm

By Joe I. Flynn

To be able to give fully of yourself, to be able to enjoy ones work or time spent at any task you're doing and be happy is truly a great gift. There are too many of us doing work we don't like. We owe to ourselves the time to get acquainted with ourselves and to know what we like and don't like, and use our likes to build talents that we can make a living with. This, in turn, will make it easier for us to become enthusiastic. The following slogan I pass on to you. The author is unknown.

ENTHUSIASM
That certain something that makes us great - that pulls us out of the mediocre and compliance - that builds into us POWER. It glows and shines, it lights up our faces -

ENTHUSIASM, the keynote that makes us sing and makes men sing with us.

ENTHUSIASM
The maker of friends - the maker of smiles - the producer of confidence. It cries to the world "I've got what it takes." It tells all men that our job is a swell job - that the house that we work for just suits us - the goods we have are the best.

ENTHUSIASM
The inspiration that makes us "Wake up and Live." It puts spring into our step - spring into our hearts - a twinkle in our eye and gives us confidence in our self and our fellow men.

ENTHUSIASM
It changes a dead pan salesman to a producer - a pessimist to an optimist - a loafer to a go-getter.

ENTHUSIASM
If we have it, we should thank God for it. If we don't have it, then we should get down on our knees and pray for it.

n News -May 1998 "Reaching Kids Over 50"

On The Lighter Side
By Joe Flynn

"ADDITIONAL HISTORY ON PLAYING CARDS"

This additional information on the history of playing cards is given because of the teriffic response received on the article I wrote, "A Deck of Cards" in March 1997. I want to add some remarks of Joseph Lemming from his book, "Tricks and Stunts with Playing Cards." He brings out that the first playing cards were probably made in China or India many thousands of years ago. From these countries card playing spread around the world.

Playing cards were not known in Europe until about 1100 AD when they were brought back by the Crusaders. These knights had found that the Saracens of Arabia were familiar with playing cards and spent many hours playing different games with them. The cards they brought back to Europe were all handmade with beautiful painted designs.

In some of these packs a variety of materials were used. In addition to paper, some playing cards were made of painted sheets of wood, ivory, metal and even dry leaves; canvas, leather and embroidered silk cards are known to have existed, as well as cards of tortoiseshell and small tiles.

Playing cards were brought to America by the sailors of the ships of the Columbus fleet but none were left here, the sailors took them all back to Spain. In 1521 Cortez in his invasion of Mexico is given credit for bringing cards to America. Many explorers brought playing cards into the New World. The invention of the printing press made it possible for the playing cards to gain general popularity.

The mystery of a deck of cards — 52 cards make a deck — and there are 52 weeks in a year. There are 13 cards to each suit — the same as the 13 lunar or moon months of each year (each have 13 weeks) making a quarter-year. There are four suits of cards in each deck: hearts, diamonds, spades and clubs, just as there are four seasons in each year.

Stop and think of all the games played with cards. The millions of card tricks one can learn, the fortunes told ... the poker games some of us should have not been in.

Life Is Such A Short Event

By Joe I. Flynn

The full realization of this comes slowly and usual toward the ending. It's toward the end of life itself that the full realization of how small a length of time it is. There was our childhood, youth, our teen years, getting an education, obtaining the right job, and there is the right woman or man to team up with. Then the task of solving the problems that life gives us, that goes with the above.

It is when we have the time or take time to analyze, look back and ask ourselves "How am I doing?". They forgot to give us written instructions when we started. Starting from scratch takes time, something that we have so little of.

My personal conclusion: It is to learn something. Learning is the key factor. There must be big challenges open, trying to understand and to remain curious about all that's taking place here and about us. We are all smarter than we're lead to believe. We all will see in time and find the true purpose for life on the planet Earth.

Yes, life is a short event.

On The Lighter Side
by Joseph L Flynn

I was bitter, and felt furious. I had this impulse to punch a coworker of mine right on the chin, to knock him out. He repeated a lie that started about me without talking about it with me. I was so upset that I got sick and had little sleep that night. This must have shown, because the next morning another of my coworkers remarked on seeing me "What happened to you?" I related the story about how the first coworker was spreading lies about me, and felt glad to get the story off my chest. On finishing, the second coworker smiled, and said, "Joe, don't you know you can't teach algebra to a dog." What he meant was that I should have known that the first coworker might be inclined to spread rumors, and that to expect something different would be like expecting a dog to learn algebra. Know thyself before you can know others. What a revelation! That did it, the shades went up, the sun came pouring in and it all made sense. My stomach felt better, I felt better, life was better.

I later discussed the matter with the coworker I was SO very mad at, told him how I felt. His first question was how could I figured a dog could not be taught algebra. He was missing the point, "Its not how smart you are its how you are smart." We often think with our emotions rather than our reasoning, or as is said, using our common sense. Knowing our strengths, and our limitations, is the first step to understanding how we can best be of service to others. It is also the key to understanding the strengths and weaknesses of others, in this case, my coworkers tendency to engage in idle gossip. If I had known myself a little better, then I might have anticipated his actions, and may have been a bit more calm when informed of his deeds.

We would not expect our dog or cat to say "Good Morning" There is a great deal of knowledge and no one knows it all, nor can they, for what is will be changed by how we see it, use it, and think about it. For what is to be learned is so vast that as we take on new knowledge, we see further and deeper. We become humbled because of the little bit we know. Even if we have twenty five master's degrees, there will always be more to learn. We learn that which interests us, which we need to get by with. So just as we realize the importance of coming to know ourselves, we must also realize that life is an endless string of changes. Things come and go, some come and are made useful after the main purpose has fallen away. In this; way we should endeavor to always be as useful as we can, knowing ourselves to know others, and adapting our skills and ability to the changes around us.

The Dillsburg Center Goes A Visiting

By Joe I. Flynn

Dillsburg Senior Center

It was not so long ago about ten of us visited the Windy Hill Center. We were welcomed, introduced, invited to be seated, and was told it was snack time. We were treated to a new type of pizza; I never had anything like it. It was sweet pizza of some kind, and it was delicious. That was a very nice welcome and I felt very much at home. The rest of the day was most enjoyable, we played some games, exchanged ideas and got to know one another. It was a very interesting day. After lunch there was a drawing and everyone received a prize.

Although this was the best there was in my visiting of other groups, there were others that came close. My thanks to all for their hospitality and goodwill. Lets say it was a half and half. When there have been larger groups, perhaps 4 or 5 centers, sometimes there have been no introductions and we were pushed in together, sat down, given food and let loose on our own. There were a number of us who did not know what was next. By the time we figured it out, the goings on were more than half over, and it was quite a let down.

It's very important that some outline be given of what's going to take place at any event, both for those volunteers who are doing the work, as well as the guests who come to the event. It's the leadership's job to keep the visitors alerted to the goings on, to keep the guests energized and captivated.

The importance of exchanging ideas, goodwill, the broadening of understanding in us all are undermined when complete introductions and ice-breaking activities are not initiated. It takes those in a leadership position to lead the program in the proper channels.

CREATIVITY BULLETIN ----- From " The Custom Man "

" Cosmetics of the Kitchen "

An open letter to all Institutional Sales People...

Knowledge of one's products increases interest, broader thinking, meaning is deepened and the product you sell becomes alive with life.

What a disappointment one finds among those who use bases on price and price alone, who have no knowledge as to the quality they are buying, no realization that they obtain only what they pay for. That when they put a cheap ingredient into the labor of cooking, their total concoction will only reflect its poorest components. Flavor is essential to any meal and the lack of knowledge by sales people makes them unable to put this point across, and in turn adds to the poor quality of their accounts.

Soup Bases are like old friends and are all too often taken for granted. These aromatic piquant and savory mixtures in bottles and pails are substances of natural orgin which when added to food, give flavor or enhance the foods own flavor, to range from everyday to the exotic.

Just as make-up can glamorize the plainest of faces soup base (cosmetic of the kitchen) adds dash and character to the most prosaic of foods. Soup bases are instant magic, for the skillful and imaginative. A little base will provide pungency and flavor, endow dishes with dash, and give character to cooking.

Never, never sell bases on price, sell the flavor, the satisfaction , the fine results. You'll be appreciated and looked up to by your accounts, not that they will always buy the best, but you'll be telling them that you want their business to remain good.

Once you sell the best base, the business is evermore yours, for once the best is used, no other will they buy. And because of the fine job you have done, competition will find it very hard to get in.

In Creative Selling,

Joe I. Flynn your "Custom Man"

(717) 697-8785

July 1999 "Reaching Kids Over 50"

Authority
By Joe I. Flynn

Webster's New World dictionary tells us "authority" is the power of right to give commands, enforce obedience, take or make final decisions.

Our congressmen and senators are elected to carry out the will of the people they represent, enacting laws for the betterment of the country. How many have forgotten the people who put them in office? Except at times when money is needed for their programs, then they think of we the people and use their authority to tax us. We should all keep in mind the importance of using authority in the proper manner and to delegate authority to a person with experience and ability, responsibility and dependability. All too often our choice is made with little thought given to the character of the individual, experience and background. We often times go along with party lines or a friend of ours and give no consideration to the many aspects that the job calls for.

This leads to poor results in the overall picture. Its effectiveness breaks down the whole process of managing things, brings about poor morale in others and waste in people's talents. Our government is noted for its waste. And we're talking about your money!

So it's well worthwhile to give thought to whom we elect to office, whom we put in charge, whom we give authority to. We may be the ones who are messing things up.

" A SALESPERSON "

A Salesperson is different things to each of us. Many think of the vacuum cleaner salesman, the used car dealer, the encyclopedia salesman or a discourtious store clerk and although this is a type of sales it's not the critique we should use when thinking of selling or salesmanship.

A Salesperson is a teacher bringing information to his trade backed by a product that has definate usefulness. Selling is a very exciting and enjoyable profession. A good salesperson likes his task and realizes nothing moves in this country until its sold.

A good Salesperson is a teacher, a scholar, a psycholgist, a pioneer. They are informed, creative, up-to-date and knows their business from a to z. A Salesperson sells ideas that promote not only the good of his own products, tangible or intangible, but is building and creating a future for his customers as well as himself for the good of all of us.

A good Salesperson working for a legitamate company not only moves merchandise or a service but brings productivity to all the members of his concern.

One should keep in mind that we are all sales people selling the greatest of all products, ourselves. The teacher sells the student, the doctor the patient, the lawyer the client, for selling is the ability to persuade, convince, break down the prejudices, get by the blocks all for the betterment of the individual or individuals concerned.

A question to ask ourselves is: How good am I at convincing or persuading someone - can I sell the idea??

Good selling is a win - win situation, all benfit!

------------joe i. flynn 6/17/85--------

The Mind Is For Thinking

By Joe I. Flynn

Some years back "THINK" signs were most popular. I remember seeing them on desks, in frames, hanging on walls in offices and other places. They made sense, for everyone thinks and we believe that the more thinking done the better the results are for the good of the whole.

I always felt there was something missing in the think signs and after giving it some thought, it came to me. It was the explanation of what thinking was or is that I was unable to recall from my schooling. I had no answer to "What is thinking?". In due time the think signs disappeared, one would have a hard job finding one today in any office or anywhere. It could be we all asked ourselves the same question. "What is thinking?".

I gave the matter some thought over the years, searching and asking, studying and reading. And the following is the explanation of thinking, I'll pass it on to you and others to see if it makes the think signs better.

Thinking is no more than making new connections with the knowledge we now have, forming a new thought. When a bit of new knowledge fits into our old the following expression is overheard, "Aha!" There is an after-feeling of "How silly of me not to see that."

We all are a lot smarter than we're given credit for or we believe ourselves to be. We all have the ability to learn to think better and we should endeavor to do so. It makes life easier for all.

A Thinking Formula - Use With Any Problem:
1. Get as many facts as you can
2. Brainstorm, get factors not necessarily related to the problem
3. Put all together, form a solution to said problem
4. Keep an open mind, keep an open mind ...

This is but a starter formula.

At Dad's burial, which was held on Father's Day, 2002, everyone had a part, which is the way Dad always liked things.

Father Waldron started the service with a reading from the bible and a few personal words.

Otto played his guitar, Joanne played her musical saw and Nick played his accordion. They played the "Prayer of St. Francis". It was absolutely beautiful.

Winifred read a passage from Ecclesiastes.

Valerie read a short reading and spoke of her memories.

Nick, Otto, Joanne, Christine and Chuck all took turns speaking.

Sandra played a tape recording of Dad from 1978. He was reciting the "Desiderata".

Joanne played "Somewhere Over the Rainbow" on her musical saw. Wonderful!

Nick brought things to a close when he played "The Big Rock Candy Mountain" on his accordion and we all sang.

We had a marvelous ceremony to say farewell.

Dad would have loved it, I'm sure.

"Your name is written on the hand of God."   Isaiah 49:16

"To live in hearts we leave behind, Is not to die."

Thomas Campbell

Joe Flynn

(As remembered by his Son-in-law, Nick Newlin, on the occasion of Joe's burial 6/15/02)

When I first met Joe Flynn, about 18 years ago, I was in the awkward position of being his daughter's boyfriend. But any concerns I had about this meeting quickly disappeared when I met Joe. He welcomed me with open arms, a hug, and a smile, with that magical twinkle in his eye that I grew to know and love so well, a twinkle that never waned or faded as long as he lived.

Joe gave me the best gift a person could give. He made me feel like anything was possible, that there was nothing I couldn't do. I was fascinated with the assortment of books he had in his basement, books on magic, mysticism, self-realization, spirituality, mind-power, and the power of positive thinking. Joe did not just own the books; he lived them, and embodied their highest principles. In all the years I knew Joe, we never had anything but positive interactions. That too was a real gift.

Joe's sense of humor was such a treat. His trademark phone greeting, "You're looking good today" never failed to tickle my funny bone. With Joe, it was that go-get'em attitude that fueled his humor, his constant writing of inspirational essays, his vivid and open-minded imagination, and his generous spirit. He touched me and so many others he shared his joy of life with.

Joe was a self- made man, an all-American success story. And he succeeded the old fashioned way: through hard work, long hours and dedication. Many is the night I would witness Joe in the office downstairs in front of his computer, working away long after lesser men had quit. He worked because he cared for the well-being and security of his family. But he also worked because it was an extension of his love for life. Joe's work, like his life, was love made visible.

And that work and love continues through the large and wonderful Flynn clan, which I'm proud and happy to be a part of. The many epic Thanksgivings, Christmases, and family reunions, full of endless amounts of food, festivity and fun continue on, as we celebrate being alive together, something Joe loved so much.

So thank you Magical Joe Flynn. I know you are up in heaven writing an essay on what it is like up there, and I feel your joy in the life ever after, as I felt your joy in your life. Godspeed, Father, Family, Friend, Joe Flynn.

Forever Young
May God bless and keep you always,
May your wishes all come true,
May you always do for others
And let others do for you.
May you build a ladder to the stars
And climb on every rung,
May you stay forever young,

Forever young, forever young,
May you stay forever young.

May you grow up to be righteous,
May you grow up to be true,
May you always know the truth
And see the lights surrounding you.
May you always be courageous,
Stand upright and be strong,
May you stay forever young,

Forever young, forever young,
May you stay forever young.
    May your hands always be busy,
    May your feet always be swift,
    May you have a strong foundation
    When the winds of changes shift.
    May your heart always be joyful,
    May your song always be sung,
    May you stay forever young,
Forever young, forever young,
May you stay forever young.

Written by ~ Bob Dylan

Talk delivered by son, John, at church service

It is an honor and a privilege for me to be here today speaking on behalf of my father, Joe Flynn.

I want to say some things that I believe about my dad and some things that my dad would have said himself if he were here.

I know right away he would have told all of you not to be sad or unhappy he is no longer here. Being the gracious man that he was, he would have thanked all of you for being here to celebrate his life, a life fully lived. Having realized so much and maybe more out of life than he may have expected, I think he would have called it a serendipitous life.

My dad told me life is like a series of plateaus. After arriving at a new plateau and learning all that there was you would then climb higher. After some struggle and effort you would arrive at another plateau, full of new ideas and experiences. Right now I believe because of the way dad lived his life and his faith in God he has reached the highest plateau.

Dad loved life and he lived it with passion. He was always ready to help with words of encouragement and inspiration. He was not only a great salesman, as a man he had no perceived limitations. Even after dealing with the symptoms of Parkinson's Disease for 20years he just kept moving forward. He never let his difficulties walking or talking diminish his inner fire. He recently told his daughter, Joanne, "I am a fortunate man." He never allowed life to compromise his dignity; self-pity was never part of my dad's recipe.

The only reason dad did not reach all his goals is because he never stopped making new ones. Just four days before he left us, my sister, Sandra, and I asked him, "How long do you want to live?" and he replied, "ninety-four."

My dad was a very optimistic man. He was a self-starter who worked long and hard. He also had a great sense of humor and loved to laugh. He gave his all at everything, always putting his best foot forward and leading by example. He believed you didn't make progress unless you stuck your neck out. He liked to think big, positive and out of the box. He believed ideas were real things because all real things are preceded by ideas.

He gave his love willingly and fully to his family. He was always there and ready to be the creative problem solver. As a dad he would sell you on your own possibilities and unlimited potential. Dad was always helpful never looking for recognition, simply watching his children grow and develop made him happy.

Family was very important to dad. He loved to be social, sitting around the dinner table talking or watching the old family movies. He reminded us all of where we came from, way back when. If you left the door open he was there to let you know, "WE AREN'T HEATING THE OUTDOORS!" If you did something wrong and there was trouble he was there and if the rough housing got to be too rough he would remind you, "THIS IS OUR HOME."

Just like my dad is helping me through this moment, I know that his influence on all of us will always be there. If my dad was here I know he would want to thank my mom for 54 years of their very happy marriage, family and personal dreams realized the exceptional care, and the undying love.

Valerie shared this reading and then some of her memories.

Aren't Birth and Death merely bookends?

When you know that you are only wearing the body, which can be destroyed, and that you are the reality which activates the body and cannot be destroyed, how can you be afraid of dying? If I believe in an existence beyond this life, why not glance at obituaries? Aren't they merely notices of a different birth?

The Desiderata

Go placidly amid the noise and haste, and remember what peace there may be in silence. As far as possible without surrender be on good terms with all persons. Speak your truth quietly and clearly; and listen to others, even the dull and ignorant; they too have their story. Avoid loud and aggressive persons, they are vexations to the spirit. If you compare yourself with others, you may become vain or bitter; for always there will be greater and lesser persons than yourself. Enjoy your achievements as well as your plans. Keep interested in your own career, however humble; it is a real possession in the changing fortunes of time. Exercise caution in your business affairs; for the world is full of trickery. But let this not blind you to what virtue there is; many persons strive for high ideals; and everywhere life is full of heroism. Be yourself. Especially, do not feign affection. Neither be cynical about love; for in the face of all aridity and disenchantment it is perennial as the grass. Take kindly to the counsel of the years, gracefully surrendering the things of youth. Nurture strength of spirit to shield you in sudden misfortune. But do not distress yourself with imaginings. Many fears are born of fatigue and loneliness. Beyond a wholesome discipline, be gentle with yourself. You are a child of the universe, no less than the trees and stars; you have a right to be here. And whether or not it is clear to you, no doubt the universe is unfolding as it should. Therefore be at peace with God, whatever you conceive Him to be, and whatever your labors and aspirations, in the noisy confusion of life keep peace with your soul. With all its sham, drudgery and broken dreams, it is still a beautiful world. Be careful. Strive to be happy.

Written in 1927 by Max Ehrmann, a poet and lawyer from Indiana.

Desiderata is Latin meaning "things desired"

Joe had recorded himself reciting the "Desiderata" back in 1978, when his voice was strong, before he had Parkinson's disease. Sandra played this at her dad's memorial service. Some could not remember his voice as it was before he was sick. It was so good hearing him speak clearly and distinctly again. I'm sure Joe was smiling down on us from heaven, because he got the last word in!

Smile...
I'm with you always,, We'll meet again someday.

Winifred read this passage from Ecclesiastes 3:1-8

There is an appointed time for everything, and a time for every affair under the heavens.

A time to be born, and a time to die; a time to plant, and a time to uproot the plant.

A time to kill, and a time to heal; a time to tear down, and a time to build.

A time to weep, and a time to laugh; a time to mourn, and a time to dance.

A time to scatter stones, and a time to gather them; a time to embrace, and a time to be far from embraces.

A time to seek, and a time to lose; a time to keep, and a time to cast away.

A time to rend, and a time to sew; a time to be silent, and a time to speak.

A time to love, and a time to hate; a time of war, and a time of peace.

BIBLIOGRAPHY

"all photos are copies of photoes belonging to the Flynn family." n.d.

Commerce, Bureau Of Marine Inspection and Navigation United Department of. "certificates of discharge." 1938-1944.

Cripple Creek, Colarado History as Gold Mining Town. n.d. 28 March 2023.

Encyclopedia, Wikipedia. *Maritime History of The United States (1900-1999).* n.d. 6 January 2010.

SS Alcoa Puritan Torpedoing. n.d. 28 January 2010.

Flynn, Joseph I. Interview. Sandra Flynn Camburn. 1998-1999.

Flynn, Joseph I, et al. "Personal Letters." n.d.

Flynn, Joseph I. "minutes from the meetings at the A.A.Seaman's Club at 36th Street New York, New York." 1946-1948.

Flynn,Joseph I. "resumes and job applications." 1948-1973.

Herbert, Brian. *The Forgotten Heroes.* New York: Tom Doherty Associates,LLC, 2005.

Miller, Kerby and Patrica Miller. *Journey of Hope.* San Francisco: Chronical Books, LLC, 2001.

Records, United Sates Personnel. *United States Marine Corps Records of Joseph Benard Flynn .* Washington D.C. , 1934-1937.

Shortridge, Bud. *Ships hit by German U-Boats During WW11.* n.d. 16 February 2010.

The Big Rock Candy Mountain/ wikipedia.org song became public domain in 2024

Desiderata.com Desiderata History article and prints by Sherrie Lovier

The Flynns 2001

www.ingramcontent.com/pod-product-compliance
Lightning Source LLC
Chambersburg PA
CBHW060401080526
44583CB00012B/420